Life Plus 2 Meters
edited by David Zetland

Aguanomics Press

Amsterdam 2016

Copyright © 2016 The Authors. All rights reserved. No part of this book may be reproduced without written permission from the (appropriate) Author *except* for attributed quotations of less than 100 words.

Typeset in New Century Schoolbook and Avant Garde with LaTeX. Cover design by Selina Fernandez-Shaw (www.kutungagrafik.com).

Please contact the editor at dzetland@gmail.com for discounts on orders of 20+ copies.

Version 1.1 (visit www.lifeplus2m.com for updates)

Publisher's Cataloging in Publication
Zetland, David, editor.

Life Plus 2 Meters / David Zetland, editor — 1st ed.
p.   cm.
Summary: "This edited volume presents a series of 29 visions by 27 authors of how we might (not) adapt to life in a climate changed world where sea levels are 2 meters higher, weather patterns have shifted, storms have grown stronger, food systems are strained, and so on. These visions take place in the future, but they are anchored in our present." — Provided by publisher.

ISBN-13: 978-0-615-57848-4

Contents

Preface: About this project   1
David Zetland

Forward: Redesign your community   3
Henk Ovink

1   School run   5
John Sayer

2   New normal extreme   9
Ilaria Meggetto

3   Last man in England   13
Sarah Dixon

4   It's about time!   19
Chris Holdsworth

5   Childhood climate dreams   23
Usha Nair

6   The not-so-friendly skies   27
David Zetland

7	Endlands Catherine Jones	31
8	Social capital as the key to adaptation Daniel Hall	33
9	The underpass Joseph Cohn	37
10	Jakarta's sinking, filthy future Roanne van Voorst	39
11	Manhattan pirates Luna Lovewell	43
12	Food needs soil John Simaika	47
13	Happy delta life Lucas Janssen	51
14	Offshore, a deep subsea well to sink Todd Jarvis	55
15	Tides will tear us apart Emma J. Myatt	59
16	Two meters of migration Binayak Das	65
17	The Century of Division Joe Cotton	69

18	Manage better, now Ralph Pentland	73
19	Bacon for everyone Philip Ridgers	77
20	Passports or people? Choose one. David Zetland	81
21	Slowly too late Majel Haugh	85
22	The beach that ate Silicon Valley Jennifer LaForce	87
23	I don't like these storms anymore Ben Ruddell	91
24	A village's uncertain future Tran Thi Kim Lien	93
25	The sentencing Annie Percik	95
26	Coastal freshwater aquifers join the sea Nazli Koseoglu	97
27	A view from dry land Clay Reynolds	101
28	A family farm in the future Kai Olson-Sawyer	105

29 The bore is coming   **109**
   Sarah Dixon

Afterword: Now what?   **113**
   David Zetland

About this project

David Zetland

I began the Life Plus 2 Meters project in August 2016 after reading Martin Weitzman's 2011 paper "Fat-tailed uncertainty in the economics of catastrophic climate change" and Hansen et al.'s 2016 paper "Ice melt, sea level rise and superstorms: evidence from paleoclimate data, climate modeling, and modern observations that 2C global warming could be dangerous" (available at www.lifeplus2m.com/science). The two papers led me to believe that our economic models severely understate the risk from climate change and that the IPCC's estimated increase in sea level ("1 meter by 2100") is far too optimistic. Hansen et al. say that sea level may rise by 6–9m by 2100. Even worse, that rise may arrive in an abrupt shock (e.g., "3–4m in a couple of years") that would make retreat, rather than adaptation, the only response.

This project aims to engage the public in planning for changes far more dramatic than those discussed in governmental and international forums, and it uses "climate fiction" methods of bringing different potential outcomes to life.

This edited volume presents a series of 29 "visions" by 27 authors of how we might (not) adapt to life in a climate-changed world where sea levels are 2 meters higher, weather patterns have shifted, storms have grown stronger, food systems are strained, and so on.

These visions may not agree with each other: their authors come from different academic, social and philosophical backgrounds. They will not be 100 percent accurate: our lives are affected by a complex mix of environmental, social, political and economic forces. They may not change your mind: everyone will read and interpret them differently. Our only goal here is that these visions help you think about how you, your community and your world — our civilization — might adapt to life in a climate-changed world.

The book is organized in chapters that alternate between storyteller and practitioner perspectives to help readers reflect on this complex topic. You can comment (or praise!) any chapter in this book — as well as see extra photos, links or references — by visiting the chapter online using the URL formula of `tiny.cc/lp2m-X` where X is the chapter number, e.g., `tiny.cc/lp2m-4` for chapter 4.

David Zetland, editor
Amsterdam
December 2016

Redesign your community

Henk Ovink

The World Economic Forum's 2016 Global Risks Report puts water crises as the top global risk for the next decade. Two billion people will be dead by 2050, four billion in 2080 if we continue with our current practices. Ninety percent of all worldwide disasters are water-related, and I could continue this list of water despair.

Global urbanization brings growth and development, but it also drives the climate change that is straining our societies, economies and ecologies. If we don't act the system will collapse, leaving us all worse off.

Water lies at the heart of this uncertain future, as it is through changes in water flows that we will feel the impact of climate change the most. Water quality defines our economic and societal prosperity, and water quantity — too much or too little — defines our societies' vulnerability. It is for these reasons that regions, cities and communities worldwide need to adapt and increase the resilience of their water management systems.

The slowness of climate change slows our response and preparation, but we have choices to make! We can choose to be transformative rather than incremental, leap-frogging our collective approaches past outdated paradigms to create robust systems that aid development while reducing the risks from climate change.

We have to start by acknowledging that complexity needs to be embraced and that design and collaboration must go hand in hand with politics and investment. Inclusive collaboration means that all layers of government will work with industry, activists, and other stakeholders. Are such hopes of cooperation too good to be true?

President Obama wanted to deliver on that promise after the devastation of Superstorm Sandy. As a member of his Hurricane Sandy Rebuilding Task Force, I developed "Rebuild by Design" to help the region's communities prepare for future uncertainties in a collaborative and innovative way. New perspectives and strong coalitions bypassed current systems to create better policies and take projects from design to reality — by design.

There is no time for free-riding or back room deals. We need innovation through an inclusive and collaborative approach. We can do it, and we must do it, as we have no time to waste!

These efforts require our imagination and desire to work together to survive and thrive as the climate changes. This book will help you imagine that future world and inspire you and your community to act together — by design.

Henk Ovink is Special Envoy for International Water Affairs for the Kingdom of The Netherlands, Sherpa to the High Level Panel on Water, and Principal of Rebuild by Design

School run 1

John Sayer

Good morning girls. Have you packed your lunches? We have some papaya from the tree beside our house, take that too. The tree's doing better since we joined the Compost Compact. We need more home-grown fresh fruit since they put that quota on air-freight food imports to Hong Kong.

You can bring your sandwich onto the ferry. That new electric boat is more stable than the old one, and nice and quiet when I feel like a nap.

Yes, you can carry your parasolas today. Don't stab other pedestrians in the eye while you're playing with them and don't damage the cells or the fans. Use them, though; the UV forecast is 'extreme' today. Wear your evapocool undershirts as well. You'll look like the plastic bottles they're recycled from!

I've got to stay in this morning, they're fitting our home air-and-water temperature system later today. Yes, hot water and cool air from the same machine. It will run off our own roof panels on a sunny day, and we sell extra electricity to Hong Kong Electric... to get a lower power bill.

While the engineers are here I'll ask when the salt water flushing system is going to be installed on the island. We are among the last districts to be fitted. Yes, most of Hong Kong's toilets were converted years ago to use sea water.

Convenient to stay home; they're doing a 'floor lift' at the office this month; moving everything out of the ground floor of our office block and knocking the walls out to allow water to pass under in case of street floods. Not too big problem for our work, I mean who in Hong Kong isn't used to the best use of small areas? Just better sharing of desk space? And perhaps more working from home.

Actually the opened up street level under our office will be made into a walk-though public space, with improved air circulation. It will probably become part of the 'cool spots' initiative — that's right, those places where people can sit in a mist breeze for a minute or two if they overheat on the streets. Yes, I do like them. Have you tried the new scented mists? Menthol, lemon, mango? I think the cosmetic companies should sponsor them! We could have an Issey Miyake mist stop, a Burberry breeze break. Perhaps Body Shop could produce a mosquito-repelling mist.

They have mist fans in the school playground don't they? All the recreation areas are covered right? When you play on the fields you wear those Foreign Legion hats don't you?

I do hope this Great Harbour Wall will help keep water levels down when it's finished. I'm glad they covered the cycle track along the top with a solar panel roof. You can cycle anywhere along the whole waterfront without getting bleached in the sun. A clever idea to add that tidal energy trial into the wall over by the old airport too — they've nicknamed it "the steel dragon" because of the bendy bits.

Did you see that the Mandatory Provident Fund are offering higher returns to anyone who cycles or walks to work? That's because they think we'll use less money on medical costs. They call it nudging I think — so know your being nudged! Well, I'll let you cycle to school when they have completed the separate track, I don't want you to go under a bus — those electric ones are a bit quiet.

What's your after-school service activity today? Outreach to help old people respond to extreme weather or flood warnings? Some use smartphones and some need a young person to go round and talk to them. That's nice for them anyway, you should plan to visit them even if they do have a smart phone; even when the weather is safe.

The school is helping with flood probability surveys?

I see, you make a record of the types of doors and windows in low-lying houses, and the direction the doors face and then this is combined with a GPS flood map to work out overall vulnerability. Do they fit those flood shields? They block the doorway, it slots into the door frame, for about half a meter. Mostly plastic, very strong, made over the border in China.

And your school community service? Mozzie watch? That's looking out for standing water isn't it? You can report people? Sounds a bit tough, they can get fined can't they? Well I suppose they've had enough warning about the rules, and the drainage services are free if work is needed. Still, children reporting adults... make sure you don't start behaving like Red Guards and tormenting adults whose minds are not as sharp as yours.

Don't forget that this weekend we're doing the Really Really Free Market in the village. You're working on ceramics, clothes and cloth. I'm on wood and furniture. I also agreed to do an hour on the Green Cottage stall with veggie breakfasts for everyone in aid of the help the Village Circular Economy initiative.

Have a nice day today. There's a typhoon out beyond the Philippines, but you've downloaded the Water Watch app right? Why do you call it 'turds'? Typhoon, tide deluge and surge; very funny — not. Alright, phone charged right? Use the elevated walkways okay! Sunblock please, parasolas or no parasolas.

Goodbye, stay safe

Bye... haven't you forgotten something? Water bottles, water bottles. Remember the trouble you got into with that plastic bottle!

No, the typhoon's still a couple of days away. You may have to have a day's skypeschool if it arrives.

John Sayer is Director of Carbon Care Asia and lives on car-free Lamma Island with two daughters who travel to school by public ferry. The Really Really Free Market and Green Cottage Café exist already and so does seawater flushing for 80 percent of Hong Kong's toilets.

Two

New normal extreme

Ilaria Meggetto

Science tells us that we should expect increased temperatures in the upcoming years and that, even if we were to suddenly cease all anthropic emissions of greenhouse gases today, the global thermometer would still go up by some points, due to the climate system's inertia, and stabilize only in the long term. As discouraging as it is, this is not the worst thing about climate change. The data we have is also consistent in indicating not only an increase in temperature records, but also an increase in their variance, so that while all temperatures rise on average, so does the frequency of their extremes and the events connected to them — droughts, floods, heatwaves and storms.

I have lived in different places, experiences hot and cold climate. Before 2013, though, I had never been to the Tropics so when I moved to South China I did know what a typhoon is but had no idea what it means. During my first week there I was awoken by a strong thundering noise, so overwhelming and continuous that it could not be ignored. They sky over the 14-million-people-megacity of Guangzhou had turned deep red and, together with the intense smog above the whole area — making the horizon smoky all the time — for a moment I was under the impression the city was being bombed. Then, all of a sudden, a violent wind carried a mountain of water down the place. The rain did not stop for 4 days. Streets flooded. Electricity failed. Typhoon Utor had landed.

A typhoon is a tropical cyclone, a storm system generated by the evaporation of massive amounts of water and it is characterized by intense thunderstorms whose winds blow above 118 km/h. As I learnt, locals call the period from May to September the "Season of Storms" and 2013 was the most active Pacific typhoon season since 2004 and the deadliest since 1975. A total of 52 depressions, 31 storms, 13 typhoons and 5 super typhoons formed in that year, the last being Category 5 Super Typhoon Haiyan that, with its winds up to 230 km/h, bought devastation across the South China Sea and 6,300 victims in the Philippines.

Understanding how this system works was crucial for me as it will be for many: deciding whether the apartment you want to rent is at risk of flood, knowing where to go when the typhoon alarm rings, stocking water supplies, putting together an emergency kit... are only some of the basic things needed to live in a place hit by intensified weather events. This situation, however, is not a local problem as it is transforming in geography and occurrence as we speak.

Oceans are warming up all over the world. The duration, intensity and number of storms has already increased by 50 percent compared to the 1970s. 70 to 100 tropical storms used to be the annual average but in the past few years this number has been almost matched by the storms generated in the North Pacific Ocean alone

Half of the world's population resides along the coast, threatened by the sea level rise and the violence of weather events. When it comes to climate talks, water scarcity is in the spotlight but where water is too much, rising above the 2-meter threshold and storming densely inhabited shores, the situation is equally dreadful. As disrupted climate patterns and unpredictable trends reach areas considered stable or safe in the past, being able to "read the signs", subscribing to weather alerts, living "prepared" is likely to become the new normal for most of us.

Ilaria Meggetto is a Project Manager at Hydroaid (Italy), researcher, traveller, and passionate about climate change.

Last man in England 3

Sarah Dixon

'Confirmation from the PharmaCo Court today, that judges have not yet made a determination in the case of Mr Ronald Balcock, the so called 'last man in England'. A decision is expected before close of business today as to whether Mr Balcock will be forcibly evacuated, or allowed to remain to face the incoming tide.'

Ty sighed. His parents were glued to the viewscreen, like all the older generation. He didn't get it. Why were they still so obsessed with what happened on Old Earth? They should move on, look to the future. That's why they'd left, after all: So there was a future.

The tablet computer in his lap showed the same footage as the viewscreen on two thirds of its display, the remaining third showed thumbnails of related vids with more information. He clicked on the top one, turning up the volume so he could hear the narration over the noise of the room.

'The PharmaCo Fleet left Old Earth on June 30th, 2045, transporting colonists from the polluted and dangerous conditions of their home world and out, to create a better life. When National and Global Government failed, the Corporations stepped in, funding the development of space craft and the colonisation of new planet—'

Ty rolled his eyes. Yes, he'd heard all that before. He glanced up and checked the room, making sure his Grandparents hadn't heard the voice over. The last thing he needed was his Grandad going off on one about how the Corporations had them over a barrel; how they were all slaves now, bought and sold. His Dad would only get angry, shouting about how freedom didn't mean a thing if you were dead.

Ty didn't get why they all got so upset about Old Earth. He knew it had been a nice place once, he'd seen

Vids of the animals and their habitats. He especially liked Tigers and Lions, and all the other big cats. The thing was though, Old Earth wasn't like that anymore. There wasn't even much left of it now, the water levels were so high. Grandad had come from England, and now there was barely enough of that left for one man to live on. Ty tapped the screen to start the next Vid.

'Who is Ronald Balcock, and why won't he leave?' a slick woman presenter said, as a picture of the old man who was the cause of all the fuss appeared on the screen.

Ty thought he looked quite nice, not a stubborn old fool like his Mum always called him. The presenter was talking about how Balcock came from a family of farmers who had always lived in the same place. That he felt a tie to the land. Fidgeting, Ty looked back up to the main screen, just in case anything had changed.

It hadn't. The cameras still showed a derelict looking farm house on the top of a hill, surrounded on all sides by water. There were evac copters circling, waiting on the order to take the man from his property. Ty huffed, sending a strand of hair puffing away from his face. Boring.

On his personal screen, the presenter was talking over some of the reasons people had given in the past for staying on Old Earth. There were a few groups who had been given permission to stay. Lunatics, Dad called them. Grandad agreed with him for some, the ones who were staying because they thought it was God's will, but not for others. The ones who agreed with him that colony life was nothing but slavery.

Ty didn't think it was slavery. They had a nice life here, a good home and plenty of food. He went to school, and he had a job all lined up for when he left too. He was contracted to work for the company, so were his kids if they didn't pay off the debt the family owed for being brought here. What was wrong with that though? They wouldn't have got here without the help from the Corporations!

The population of Old Earth was now just a few

thousand people. Cranks and crazies, clinging on to the past in the high places, his Mum said. She always sounded sad about it, though.

A noise alerted Ty to a change on the main screen, and he tapped pause on his own device to give it his full attention. One of the evac copters had flown down and landed outside of Balcock's house. The old man came out of his front door, waving his arm in a clear gesture that he wanted them to leave but the uniformed officers of Corporate Enforcement didn't take the hint.

The screen cleared without warning, the camera view changed to a first person perspective; the camera of the officer approaching the house. The wind sounded fierce through his microphone, and Ty leaned forward on his seat as he got a close up view of the terrible conditions of Old Earth.

'Get away! Leave me alone!' Balcock was shouting.

'Mr Balcock, The PharmaCo Court has instructed me to ask you a series of questions. Your answers will be live broadcast to the court and serve as your testimony where it will be used to determine whether you may remain on their property.'

'It's not their property!' Balcock argued. 'It's mine, my families! Always has been.'

The officer ignored him and carried on, 'Mr Balcock, do you believe that it is the plan of a higher power that you remain here?'

'No!'

'Mr Balcock, do you believe that humanity is a contagion that should be confined to earth?'

'No!'

'Mr Balcock, are you a member of any group which has been granted legal permission to remain on Old Earth?'

'No!'

'Mr Balcock, do you identify yourself with FirstEarth?'

Ty pricked up his ears at that question. FirstEarth were a group of terrorists, they carried out attacks in the colonies because they were so angry about the Corporations helping people get away.'

'No, you bloody idiot! Why don't you stop asking questions and just... go away?'

'Mr Balcock, do you have any comments for the court to support your decision to remain here in the light of the clear and present danger to your life by the rising water levels and atmospheric pollution?'

The old man switched in a moment from being angry and aggressive to a slump shouldered rag doll.

'Fights gone out of him,' Grandma said quietly.

The family fell silent, all other screens muted as they watched the drama unfolding on the main viewscreen.

'This is my home,' Balcock said, his voice breaking. 'A man should have the right to remain in his home, to die there if he wants to. You don't have a right to just take me away from the place I love. My heart's here.'

'Your heart?' the officer asked, puzzled.

'My whole life, my memories...' tears formed in the old man's eyes, his voice breaking. 'My wife. My wife is buried in the back garden. Please... please don't make me leave her. I just want to stay here. I'm not bothering anyone.'

Ty watched, frozen, as the old man fell to his knees and sobbed. He'd never seen a grown up cry like that before. It made him feel uneasy. He looked around the room for comfort from his family, and saw tears were rolling down all their cheeks too.

'I think that concludes Mr Balcock's testimony,' the officer snapped, and the camera cut back to the long view. The old man appeared tiny, knelt before the large man in his bulky uniform.

'And now we wait for the Court's decision,' the news presenter said smoothly. 'Balcock has received invitations from all of the groups legally allowed to remain on Old Earth but he has refused them all. He has made no statement as to why, but we presume it is because of this man's extraordinary attachment to his native land.'

Silence fell then, only the whirring noise of the evac copters as they continued to circle the building. Ty wriggled over on the sofa to sit closer to his Mum who wrapped an arm around him and pulled him in tight.

'And the Court's decision is in! Mr Balcock will be forcibly evacuated from his property for his own safety.'

His Grandparents exploded into angry words, his Father immediately arguing with them. They all spoke at once so Ty couldn't make out what was being said, but in any case, his attention was focused on the screen.

The Corporate Enforcement Officer seemed to be speaking to Mr Balcock, but the old man was still knelt down and shaking his head. The Officer pulled a weapon from its holster at his waist, checked a setting and then leveled it at the old man. He said something else, and Ty wondered why they weren't playing the audio this time. Then there was a dull, popping noise and the old man slumped to the ground.

Immediately the officer moved towards him, checking his pulse and then signalling to the copter. More officers came out with a stretcher, loading Balcock onto it and carrying him back towards their craft.

'Well, that's it then,' said Grandpa. His voice was cracked; his cheeks damp with tears. 'Last man in England, and he's gone.'

'God bless him,' muttered Grandma.

Ty rested his head against his mother and watched, hearing her let out her own sad sigh. She kissed him on the top of the head and gave him a squeeze as she whispered, 'Last man in England...'

Sarah Dixon is a prolific writer of short stories where wonder plays an important role. A wife and mother of two, it was the desire to write stories that challenged the lure of video games that led her to write her first children's novel.

Four

It's about time!

Chris Holdsworth

The single biggest barrier to our understanding about climate change is time. Time dictates everything in our lives, from our day-to-day schedules, to how our planet regulates itself, but our perception of time is entirely subjective. The recent film Interstellar beautifully demonstrated this concept, and it is something that is at the core of the discussion surrounding climate change. Where is the evidence? Why can't I see it? Why isn't it warmer? Why aren't cities underwater? To the human eye climate change is often invisible because it is planetary processes responding to human activity. The problem is that the planetary responses operate on a geological or planetary timescale, something that far exceeds our concept of time. A useful method of illustrating this is to consider the entire history of Earth in 24 hours. Do this and humans first appeared on the planet at 23:58:43, in fact industrialisation took place only seconds ago.

Herein lies the problem with climate change. It is a problem that is of our own doing, but the visible consequences far-outdate a single generation. That said, we live in a human world that operates on human timescales, and the impacts of climate change need to be assessed on these human terms. A world where sea levels are two metres higher than today is concerning, not least because research increasingly suggests this could be a possibility by the turn of the century. This is because of the complex interconnectivity of our planet's natural regulatory systems, whereby one change in the colour of a surface can fundamentally change the amount of energy available to weather systems or geochemical processes. Our planet regulates itself through a multitude of complex feedback processes, processes that we are forcing and changing at a rate rarely seen throughout Earth history. But again, we live in a human world therefore we must consider the problems that human society will encounter. Professor Brain Cox highlighted this recently:

> "The key point is can we respond to it (the clear evidence that our climate is changing). Do we have the political institutions, the political will and the organisation globally to respond to this challenge, and that worries me immensely. I don't think we do at the moment."

This is the real danger of climate change. These changes are not terminal for the Earth, it has survived much worse than us and will likely long out-live us. Climate change is humankind making its way of life and day-to-day existence much more difficult than it currently is. What Professor Cox highlights is that to change this our governance systems and figureheads need to be concerned and proactive about this issue, and right now that is simply not the case.

The idea of sea levels being two metres higher than they currently are has a certain element of Catch-22 about it. There would be no reasonable way of ignoring the problem because the visual evidence would be undeniable, particularly in government centres like London that would likely be at least partially submerged. However if we reach that extent of sea level rise we will likely be beyond the point of easily reversing the changes we have set into motion, and this is again because of how our planet regulates itself. It is if you like similar to approaching a waterfall in a boat. Turn the boat a safe distance from the waterfall edge and the financial and physical cost will be minimal, but the longer you wait and closer you get to the waterfall's edge the more difficult it becomes to reverse the direction of the boat. Wait too long and the boat tumbles over the edge, and the financial and physical cost exponentially increase, removing any real control you have in reversing the direction of the boat.

It is all rather depressing. Infuriating too because governments, particularly following the financial crash of 2008, are extremely prudent with government spending for fear of increasing national deficits and decreasing public popularity. The longer we delay in truly addressing the causes and threats of climate change, the costlier it becomes to everyone, not just government budgets. What is arguably even more tragic is the challenges of climate change present an opportunity to protect and empower individuals, particularly the most vulnerable in our societies. Small-scale, individually-owned energy production. A more regular exposure to the natural world. Enhancing the world we live in rather than degrading it. These are all part of the solution to this problem, yet we refuse to seize the opportunities it presents.

It is perhaps fitting then to finish on the news that at the end of August 2016 a specially commissioned group of scientists came to a unanimous decision that the Earth has now entered a new geological time epoch. An epoch in geological time is shorter than a 'period', but longer than an absolute date or event. A new epoch is marked by a rapid change in species numbers, radioactive particles, atmospheric temperatures and rates of erosion in the rock record. The scientists found that rapid change is taking place in all of these criteria, hence agreeing that the Earth has indeed entered a new epoch known as the Anthropocene. The transition into this new epoch from the previous one, known as the Holocene, likely took place in the mid 20th century upon the dawn of nuclear weapon usage and exponential population growth. What is even more shocking is that many scientists believe we are currently living through the sixth major mass extinction event in Earth history, the famed extinction of the dinosaurs being one of the other extinction events in Earth history. At current rates three-quarters of species could become extinct in the next few centuries because of the impact of human activity upon the Earth.

Despite all this the question remains, can we respond? Do we have the foresight and the will to effectively tackle this problem head-on and save ourselves substantial financial and social expenditure in the future? Only time will tell. There is incredible potential and opportunity to change things that will benefit all, but right now the forecast is bleak.

Chris Holdsworth is a student at The University of Glasgow where he studies Earth Science and is regularly involved in public outreach and science communication work.

Childhood climate dreams 5

Usha Nair

Harsha looked out of the window. She could see a gale building up. Trees were swaying in the wind. The noise of waves crashing against the shore some distance away could be heard clearly. She sighed and tried to keep down the fear building up inside her. This could be the beginning of yet another bad period when they would be restricted within the four walls, scared to step out and forever weary of the giant waves and sea surge that had marked previous instances of such weather. She had read in her Class VI textbook that sea levels were predicted to rise by two meters by end of the century.

The year was 2030. Harsha recalled how her mother recounted stories of her own childhood when they enjoyed the rains, running out to get drenched in the downpour and get scolded on return. Rains were regular and moderate. There was a pattern in weather events and events round the year could be predicted fairly accurately. Schools reopened after the summer vacations to torrential monsoon rains. Festival season was filled with flowers, fruits and pleasant weather. Summer was hot and humid but not too hot to run out and play through the day. What fun they seemed to have had when the whole extended family assembled at the family home in the village for school vacations!

Her father regaled them with stories about his feats in the village pond and river. He and his friends used to spend hours splashing in the water and racing each other across the wide river. But the river she saw was only a small trickle of smelly water, waylaid with lumps of unfriendly grass and mounts of sand and rock.

The family had paid short visits to their village when she was a little girl. But the journey always left bad memories, plagued by water scarcity, swarming mosquitoes and inclement weather. Over the years they had stopped undertaking those visits, much to the regret of her mother. Harsha particularly remembered the vibrant colours of the butterflies her aunt had told her about. She had only seen a rare butterfly in the park, that too in dull monotonous colours. Where have the colours disappeared? How dull and dreary her childhood seemed when compared to the lively, peppy childhood of her parents and grandparents! Who had taken away all the fun and frolic? She wished something could be done to restore the old life.

Harsha ran to her grandfather and plagued him with questions and doubts. He explained to her how Man's reckless activities over decades and centuries had destroyed the environment. Chasing the dreams of riches, comfort and enjoyment, Man went about exploiting Nature's resources without giving anything back. Slowly, ominously, the balance of Nature crumbled. Natural resources were plundered and fragile species made extinct. Natural protection for lands and seas (such as, coral reefs and mangrove forests) were destroyed in the name of development, leaving them open to danger and destruction. Climate changed all over the world. The world now faced extreme events, unprecedented heat and cold, destructive deluges and fearful sea surges.

"But, Grandpa," exclaimed Harsha, "if Man is responsible for all this, surely he can try to undo the destruction too, can't he?" Her grandfather nodded his head, "Some of the damage is unfortunately irreversible. But the good news is that Man has realised his grave mistakes and is already trying to restore some element of harmony and beauty in nature." He explained that all the countries of the world got together at the turn of the century to discuss the serious implications of the recklessness of Man. There were scientific studies and political negotiations. Before too long everyone realised that climate change is the biggest threat ever faced by humanity. It respected no divisions of prosperity, education, social status or religious belief. All people and all countries were equally affected and were destined to suffer the consequences. They realised that unless everyone joined hands and worked really hard, this calamity could not be avoided. Good sense prevailed upon the leaders of all the countries — developed, developing, under-developed — who resolved to take urgent steps necessary to keep the threat of global destruction away.

Countries took urgent steps to reduce their carbon emissions through safe energy, improved designs of buildings and vehicles, managing and protecting water resources, altering luxurious life styles with huge carbon footprints, making towns, cities and villages safe and healthy for people, ensuring sufficient food for all etc.

Now scientists say that all this has helped in bringing down emissions of harmful gases. They were looking forward to a carbon neutral world very soon. The years leading upto 2030 had seen countries pursuing development in more responsible ways, taking care to keep the methods safe and nature friendly. Of course, developing and less developed countries had to pursue some traditional methods and patterns, but they too had crossed the level of peak emissions and had started showing a sloping trend.

Harsha smiled with relief. She felt assured that her generation could look forward to a better world, a world in which there are colourful butterflies and meandering rivers. A world in which they can run around and enjoy the rains and play to their heart's fill in parks and gardens. In her heart she thanked the older generation who had shown the wisdom and good sense to arrest the journey to doom by taking action with unity. At the same time she felt a sense of responsibility. It is up to children like her to make sure that the world does not fall back into the crevice of destruction and degradation of nature. They have to be vigilant and caring, to keep Mother Earth from again facing the inhumane treatment she had been subjected to in the past. She resolved to talk to her friends and spread the word about our precious earth and its bounty, and the need to preserve and protect them at all costs.

Usha Nair is a voluntary social worker who is engaged in climate change related work. She is the Member-in-charge (Climate Change) at All India Women's Conference, a 87-year old national women's organisation in India.

Six

The not-so-friendly skies

David Zetland

The 2010 eruption of Iceland's Eyjafjallajökull volcano led to the cancellation of flights in 20 countries and delays for 10 million passengers. The interruptions highlighted our dependence on moving people and things by air. The economic loss from 7 days of cancelled flights totalled approximately 1.7 billion USD. Thankfully, nobody was killed by high winds, low visibility or increased air pollution.

My girlfriend and I experienced a different kind of delay in December 2013 when Dallas airport was closed down by unexpected snowfall. Our trip from Vancouver to the Galapagos was saved, thankfully, by rerouting via Miami.

Air travel has a disproportionate impact on climate change because its GHG emissions occur at high altitudes, but air travel also brings disproportionate benefits to many. Most people in the developed world fly to do business, see family, and enjoy vacations. The falling cost of air travel means that many people in developing countries are joining them.

The sad news is that the delays and dangers of air travel are going to increase in the future. Although Life Plus 2 Meters is unlikely to mean more volcanic eruptions, it is going to deliver similar interruptions in a different pattern. Increasing GHG concentrations are warming the Earth's atmosphere and oceans at different rates. Changed heat patterns are affecting the rate of glacial melting and the circulation of water between the ocean's surface and depths. Those impacts are, in turn, affecting the mighty currents that circulate water between the tropics and polar regions. Hansen et al (2016) predict — based on models, paleoclimate evidence, and extrapolation of current ocean temperatures and currents — that the Atlantic meridional overturning circulation (AMOC) will slow and shut down in the next few decades. The AMOC — by moving water from the Caribbean to the North Atlantic — modulates temperatures and storms in the North Atlantic. We can expect, therefore, more extreme temperatures and storms without the AMOC.

Colder winters and stronger storms will force humans, activities and infrastructure into unfamiliar territory. Impacts will be felt at all levels and sectors of society as weird weather disrupts agriculture, tests heating and power infrastructure, stresses ecosystems, and forces people to revisit habits of work and life, but the rest of this chapter will focus on air travel.

Temperature extremes are going to disrupt and endanger air travel. In northern latitudes, planes will need to de-ice more often, airports will face more snow and ice, and softer materials — everything from rubber to human skin — will need to be protected or replaced. More, stronger storms will increase risks from lightning strikes, floods and updrafts that will make it harder for planes to maneuver, take-off, fly and land. The situation might be worse in the tropics if hurricanes and rising sea levels attack airports from above and below.

Strained and broken equipment and systems will increase danger for passengers, so flight schedules will need to be padded to cope with delays and cancellations. These changes will add to the cost of air tickets as well as the risk of travel. Airports in poorer areas may have to shut down if adaptation is too expensive, increasing social distance and economic inequality.

People will cope in different ways. Virtual business meetings will become more common, family reunions less frequent. Deaths will increase from current levels (117 per billion journeys, better than motorcycles but worse than cars) to higher levels. Innovations in technology and best practices will reduce or perhaps even overcome these losses, but perfect storms of bad conditions will surprise and kill us. Runways will buckle or crumble into sinkholes, short-circuits will leave planes blind, turbulence will turn planes into roller coasters.

Liquid fossil fuels are particularly well suited for flying, so they are unlikely to be replaced by sustainable alternatives, but that detail is unlikely to matter to people worried about iced jets chopping through turbulence to land on a runway that may hide a fatal pothole. The future of flying is more likely to be affected by outside changes that make the skies not-as-friendly to fly.

David Zetland is an assistant professor at Leiden University College, where he teaches various classes on economics. He blogs on water, economics and politics at `aguanomics.com` *and founded the "Life Plus 2 Meters" project.*

Endlands

Catherine Jones

flickering greys, the sea
changes: unaltering,
silently, chivvies, switching
the soft primrose sand; one
grain flicks position with
another — impossible, inevitable.

the boats are silent — they
cross this expanse at the end of lands
vikings first, then pirates
raid and burn, settle and farm,
netherlanders, flatland explorers,
hunting the new crossings, echo
the dykes and drains- invisible tracks,
eat their way into the soft marshes,
expose the rich peats,
carve and create out of nolands.

inlets creeks and badlands,
flatlands perfect
for creeping smugglers lands
illicit acts in shifting edges
land of no land
sea of no sea

   estuary

but the sea can rise,
crawl towards the sky,
the moon cries, desires,
dragging it over land hand made land

water
energetically, without mercy,
rushes over the flatlands,
washes away the coastlands,
demolishes all in its pathlands,
creates new edgelands —

nomanslands

Catherine Jones is a musician, writer and artist who studied and lived 8 years in the East Anglian fens and flatlands. Much of her writing harks back to her memories of living and working in an unstable environment.

Eight

Social capital as the key to adaptation

Daniel Hall

Current climate change policy is aimed primarily at mitigation, to reduce the greenhouse gases causing it. Environmentalists use a sustainability argument that we should not further deplete earth's ability to assimilate carbon capacity to the point of damaging future generations. Yet efforts have not been significant enough to come even close to sustainability in this sense.

Economics Nobel Laureate Robert Solow gives a broader definition of "sustainability" in his article, "Sustainability: An Economist's Perspective". He argued that sustainability does not necessarily involve protecting a particular resource or natural way of life and that sustainability can mean not leaving future generations with a lower capacity to meet their general needs. This opens a role for adaptation in addressing climate change. People often think of the greenhouse gas problem as a pollution problem, but it can also be thought of as an extraction of the atmospheric and oceanic carbon-absorbing services of the earth. We are depleting this 'natural capital' to extract profits ("rents") via market goods today. Solow said that sustainability can also be applied to the depletion of a nonrenewable resource if we properly invest the resource rents in activities conducive to economic growth and finding substitute resources.

Responsible policy involves accepting that we have already caused significant climate change and start using the rents from our depleted natural capital (the assimilative capacity) to invest in adaptation capital. We will need physical capital to rebuild and repurpose our infrastructure in adaptation to climate change. We will need human capital to solve challenges we will fail to anticipate. Finally, we will need social capital to collectively meet the challenges climate change will bring us.

Social capital is a measure of trust, cooperation, and participation in community and society. What if climate change makes where you live undesirable? If you had to relocate, who could help you move? Who would give you a place to stay outside your family when they have to move too? Who will bring you food and other necessities when the supply chains running to your house are temporarily broken? Will we engage in conflict over our reduced resources, or will we cooperate in the management of their scarcity? With rising temperatures, rising sea levels, and rising frequency and severity of disasters, our public and private sector support systems will be overwhelmed. We will need social capital to address these problems in a quick and decentralized manner.

Unfortunately, there is already insufficient investment in social capital today. People are joining organizations less and volunteering with groups less (Putnam 1995). When a large disaster like Hurricane Katrina or more recently Hurricane Matthew hits and captures media attention, we manage to pool our resources and find a way to help those most damaged. With extreme climate change these disasters will happen so frequently that we will become desensitized, then disaffected, then overwhelmed, and finally too busy saving ourselves to help others. We cannot wait to build social capital when cooperation becomes more challenging after climate change happens.

How can we reinvest in social capital? First, communities must commit to do so, and if viewing social capital as a form of adaptation capital serves as a catalyst, great. Businesses need to encourage employees to join organizations and participate in community activities. Government can provide incentives for donating time and talent as they do for charitable donations. Volunteer associations and non-profits must modernize and equip their organizations to anticipate and handle the future needs. Everyone can get to know their neighbor and help each other address problems.

Adaptation will require cooperation, and by building our cooperative capacities today, perhaps we can get closer to sustainability after severe climate change.

Daniel Hall is an Assistant Professor of Economics at High Point University in North Carolina. He serves HPU and community at large as the advisor to the Civitan Club on campus, a group known for good works and civic duties.

The underpass 9

Joseph Cohn

The storm raged all night. The refugees trembled as the wind howled beneath the bridge. Soon the water rose. For two hours it roared through the underpass. Along the concrete walls black shapes writhed in the primordial darkness. The underpass became a vault of screams to echo the agony of the dying earth. By dawn the flooding had ended and thirty-three people had died.

In the morning the refugees climbed down to scavenge and search for the dead. They cleared the ground and sent the dead into the sea, and then they gathered to eat out of cold, dented cans. Afterward they rested against the walls and watched the world with mute eyes. Their figures faded into the gloom, until they were no more than shadows of anguish. No one spoke, and no children ran at play. The last child living beneath the bridge had died three weeks ago.

Around midday a wild-eyed man with long, tangled hair stood at the center of the underpass. From a ragged book he read to the refugees of prophets and dead kings and a time when the earth burned. But above all else he spoke of an empire called Babylon. Of how it fell at the height of glory, its towers and walls crumbling to the earth. The refugees heard him, but they did not listen.

A month later the underpass was silent and the people were gone. Whether they fled to some distant Elysian field or perished beneath the bridge was unknown. Their fates like their origins were lost, their existences forgotten. All was still but for the ocean. It loomed just beyond the bridge, gray and calm and ever shifting. A mercurial plain beneath whose surface lay the ruins of Babylon. A sepulcher fit to house all human folly.

Joseph Cohn is a high school student from Southern Cal-

ifornia. Growing up close to the ocean, he has seen how all human activities — ranging from fishing to littering — can harm our oceans.

Ten

Jakarta's sinking, filthy future

Roanne van Voorst

According to the politicians working in Jakarta, Indonesia's megacity capital, this city is turning into 'the place to be'. By 2018, they promise that a city known for its slums, floods and garbage will be '100 percent slum free, flood free and garbage free'. It will thus be clean, modern and attractive for both inhabitants and visitors, who might especially enjoy the green running tracks that will have been developed alongside formarly clogged rivers, and the seaside residential neighbourhoods in the North, where one can shop and live in style. Ideally, Jakarta's great transformation will be complete by 2018 (when the Asia Games take place in the city), but there may be some work left to do.

As unrealistic as these announcements may seem to people who have visited Jakarta, they should by no means be considered hollow phrases. The current generation of politicians in Jakarta don't just talk; they are actually getting things done. Everybody who has recently visited the city will have noticed that politicians, advisors and developers are making enormous efforts to change Jakarta's negative image. Slums have been torn down; roads have been constructed; Dutch water experts are building a 32 km-long wall to protect the Northern coast from a rising sea; programmes have been initiated to dredge garbage from canals; parks have been created; and run-down colonial houses are being demolished and replaced by Grande Plazas.

So the problem is not that nothing happens in Jakarta. The problem is that what is happening is of no use because none of these programs address the root causes of Jakarta's challenges. The sad fact is that Jakarta's future is more likely to include more, larger floods, deeper poverty for slum residents, and tides of feces flowing past seaside villas. The impacts of climate changes — more rainfall and rising sea levels — might make you think of Jakarta as 'the city you definitely want to avoid' in the future.

Let me give some context to that rather gloomy vision. Jakarta's already serious flooding problems are caused by multiple factors, of which urban mismanagament is perhaps most important. For decades, politicians have prioritized commercial developments over public services. The lack of an effective garbage collection system means that most households dump their rubbish in the rivers. Affordable housing shortages have led the city's poor to build their houses in the river's flood plains. Only half of households receive piped water, so everyone else pumps groundwater. The resulting land subsidence means the city is sinking by 3 to 20 cm per year — a problematic trend even before considering the additional danger of sea levels that are rising by 6 mm per year in Jakarta Bay. Finally, remember that falling groundwater and land elevations are damaging the city's drainage, drinking water and sewerage systems.

The current trend towards short-term, superficial solutions might seem to be improving the city's livability, but they are merely sweeping real problems under the carpet. These problems can be solved, but solutions demand long-term political commitments to providing piped water, sewerage, and social housing.

Building a wall to protect from sea level rise will not help if the land continues to subside. Dredging canals will not protect the city from flooding if people continue to live where the river needs to flood and dump their garbage in canals. New villas will not provide safe and glamorous lifestyles if rising rivers dump faeces and garbage on their lawns.

Roanne van Voorst is a postdoctoral researcher at Erasmus University, The Hague, the Netherlands. She wrote her PhD dissertation on responses of slum dwellers in Jakarta, Indonesia to the risks of recurrent floods and evictions.

Manhattan pirates   11

Luna Lovewell

From nearby balconies, the men at the guns cheered as The Stork came sailing down 7th Avenue loaded with new cargo. Children scrambled across the makeshift bridges and ropeways to follow the boat heading towards the docks over what used to be Washington Square Park. Captain Andrews was one of the few men old enough to remember what it had looked like before the floods. The lively mix of tourists, intoxicated college students, and wealthy yuppies. The blaring taxi horns, live music, and just the general hustle and bustle of life in New York city. Now it was silent except for the waves lapping against crumbling buildings and the call of gulls from overhead.

As soon as the ship was tied up, the forlorn docks sprang to life. Men who'd been desperate for work seemed to just materialize out of thin air until there was a whole horde of them helping to unload each and every box. There had once been a pretty stable trade in salvaged goods around here, but the slowly dying industry had fallen from its last leg over the past year or so. The most easily accessible parts of the city had been pretty much picked clean of everything useful, and the new cities on dry land had begun to manufacture their own goods again. So traders with no goods and no market were forced to find a new career in piracy.

"Where'd you go?" One of the boys called. Captain Andrews recognized the young Robinson boy; that face full of freckles was unmistakeable. "You go to the Mississippi Bay?" Though it was a long trip from New York, it was a popular destination for the other crews due to the booming trade between the Appalachian and Rocky cities. Trade ships were plentiful, but so were naval ships ready to blow pirates out of the water.

Andrews shook his head and grinned. "East, my boy!

The settlements in the Pyrenees are producing like you wouldn't believe!"

"Any fruit?" called out a woman from the docks. "Citrus?" A whole chorus of other women clustered around, eager to also hear the answer. They'd managed to start growing beans and a few other crops on some of the skyscraper roofs, but anything with a decent amount of Vitamin C refused to grow here. Scurvy affected nearly every family.

"Sorry, no citrus. But lots of other foodstuffs, including some fresh meat!" That got a rousing cheer from the men scrambling across the docks with heavy boxes; livestock wasn't a common sight in NYC nowadays, and as a former fishing vessel, The Stork was one of the few ships left in the city with a refrigerated cargo hold.

Captain Andrews turned to his first mate. "Make sure it all gets accounted for," he said. What kind of pirate would he be if the dock crew was able to steal the same goods that he'd already stolen. "And get it to market as soon as possible. I'm going home."

"Ay, sir." He would have liked to return to his wife too, but that's the benefit of being captain and not first mate.

Captain Andrews made his way toward Midtown, through the markets of vendors all selling the same rusted appliances and useless knick-knacks. He stopped to chat a few times, having gotten to know most of the city's merchants through various dealings over the years. But they lost interest in the conversation with him when they learned that the first mate would be distributing the cargo. Just as well; he had better things to do than talk to them.

Finally Captain Andrews arrived home. After nearly 2 months at sea, he was eager to stretch his legs and bolted up the concrete stairs toward the apartment. It was a posh penthouse that overlooked the flat square of water that used to be Central Park. Someone very wealthy had once owned this place, and they'd no doubt evacuated to their second home in Vail or Gstaad or some other mountain destination when the floods came. But it served well for Captain Andrews and his family.

His wife rushed to put her arms around his neck, and his daughter came toddling into the atrium shortly after. He scooped the little girl up in a hug and held them both tight. "I've missed you both so much." And from his pocket, he withdrew the prize that he'd hidden even from his own crew. A perfect, fat, juicy orange that he'd taken off of the captain of the ship they'd robbed off the coast of what used to be France. Just the smell of it had nearly driven Captain Andrews mad on the way back across the Atlantic, but it was totally worth it to see both of their faces light up. "This is for you."

Luna Lovewell (aka W.P. Kimball) writes often on reddit, where this piece originally appeared. She has published a collection of her stories as [Prompt Me].

Twelve

Food needs soil

John Simaika

As seen from space, we live on a blue planet — a planet full of water — with a little green and brown here and there. A closer look, however, reveals that especially around coasts, there is often a brown soup coming from streams entering the ocean, for example off the east coast of Madagascar. The majority of times, this is associated with land use, starting far upstream of the wide rivers that then carry once fertile soils, accumulated over hundreds of kilometers, into the oceans. A lot of this soil will have been washed into streams by a process known as erosion, the natural enemy of soil formation. Erosion can be water-based or wind-based. In most cases, water erosion is of concern. In a world where the weather is predicted to become more extreme, soil erosion by water will, for many reasons increase significantly.

But why should we care about `dirt'? Well, because dirt is alive, an ecosystem of its own, that is so diverse, that it carries a plethora of organisms in just a teaspoon. In that teaspoon will be bacteria and fungi, part of the so-called microfauna, and nematode worms, mites and springtails, to name a few of the larger mesofauna. This might not seem all that significant, but soil ecosystems are responsible for the global storage and release of CO_2, a greenhouse gas known to cause global climate change. It is the capacity of soils overall to store carbon that aids in mitigating climate change, but this capacity, and its response to a changing climate is not yet well understood. With limits on time for action, soil conservation and the creation of carbon sinks or pools is high on policy agendas.

Apart from their role in climate change mitigation, soils are responsible for good plant growth and thus maintain animal life, including human life. Soil quality, topography and microclimate are essential ingredients to plant crop health and thus good quality food. The effects of climatic change on soil per se are complex, as they depend on soil type (the physical composition), topography, biological soil composition (those little microbes and invertebrates mentioned earlier), ecosystem type (for example grassland or forest), local climate, the direction of rainfall change, land use and land management.

Rainfall patterns and intensity in particular, are a direct concern: While areas that are already dry are predicted to become drier, those that are wet are becoming wetter still. The real concern is with the intensity of rainfall events. Fewer rainfall days are predicted, with more rainfall overall, in those days. It is the intensity of the rainfall that causes more soil to erode quicker. In a warmer, wetter world, rates of soil erosion will therefore increase. Already, in Europe, the mean soil loss rate (2.2 tons/ha-year for non-erosion-prone areas) exceeds the average soil formation rate (1.4 tons/ha-year) by a factor of 1.6. About 12.7 percent of arable land in the European Union experiences unsustainable rates of soil loss (>5 tons/ha-year), a pattern which is considered a major threat to food security for the European Union. Factoring in more intense rainfall events in the future, would translate to higher incidences of crop damage and to even greater losses of soils and carbon stocks across greater agricultural landscapes.

With about 11 billion people to feed, agriculture will have to intensify, presumably on smaller pockets of land, as increasingly erosion and salinization take their toll on the landscape. Anti-erosion measures will have to be implemented such as reduced or no tillage, the planting of cover crops, keeping plant residues at the soil surface, the maintenance of stone walls, and the increased use of grass margins and contour farming. Urban populations will have to adapt, and new innovative ways of making food in cities will have to take precedence. Urban agriculture might take the shape of roof-top and balcony gardens, and hydroponic installations. Urban gardens and public parks could also increasingly play a role in food security, as they will be increasingly used to grow food. It could also mean that our reliance on high impact foods such as red meat will have to take a backseat to eating insects. Food production in the city would not only add utilitarian value, but potentially decrease greenhouse gas emissions and improve air quality, while increasing the aesthetic appeal of city life, where at least some people would experience a sense of place and being.

John P. Simaika is a Conservation Ecologist at the Department of Soil Science, Stellenbosch University. His research is applied, focusing predominantly on the conservation of insects in land- and waterscapes.

13

Happy delta life

Lucas Janssen

Note from the editor: In the past months, during our *Futurum Urbanum* editorial meetings we came to the conclusion that we should also pay attention to developments beyond the scope of the metropole. Statistics show that there is a growing number of people that exchange their city life for a living on the countryside. This tendency can be recognized in the whole European continent. In the editorial board we wanted to understand why people make such choices. Therefore, we visited a small community in the eastern part of the Netherlands, where we had an interview with Mark van der Steen (44). Mark and his family live in Honderdmorgen, a community quite close to the Waal river. This interview was originally published in our November 2036 edition.

FU: Why did you decide to move to Honderdmorgen?

Mark: At first, we lived in Amsterdam. It is the city everybody wants to live in, and so did we. After some years we started to experience that it was not really that great. First of all, we had great difficulties in finding good education for our three children. The situations in the schools were really bad and good teachers missing. And then, of course, there were the climate effects. During summer, every two weeks we had a flooding leading to a total congestion of the city. The summer heat and the growing number of insects made it hard to be outside.

FU: How did you end up here?

Mark: Well, we were scanning the various options in the Dutch countryside as we wanted to make a living in production of high quality food. In this area the prices had significantly dropped because of the expectations of continuous flooding from the Rhine, or Waal as this branch is called. There were a lot of deserted houses. Hence, the prices were low and we decided to take a chance. Apart from the lower areas there are also some higher grounds in this area.

FU: And how did it work out?

Mark: In the end it worked out quite well! We are here now for almost eight years. We have a real nice community of nine families that make a living with the production of food and we have been able to organise the education for our children. In terms of flooding, after a couple of years it turned out differently. Germany introduced their 'Wasserwende'. They started retaining their water by building large reservoirs and infiltration works. As a result, we have not been flooded since we are here. Actually, we need to take various measures to have sufficient water to farm here such as closed reservoirs. One of the unexpected is that truffles are growing in the higher located forests.

FU: So what is it actually that you make a living with?

Mark: There is quite a large group of people in cities that want high quality foods. We produce a wide variety of meat, vegetables and fruits. The vegetables and fruits are of course seasonal; the meat is sold continuously. We raise the 'Roman Roosters', which are sold in cities across the border as well. Chefs like the meat of our roosters because of its intense taste and nice structure. For the fruits, for instance, we are growing seven varieties of raspberries as well a three varieties of gooseberries.

FU: This all sounds... almost Arcadian. At the same time I can imagine there must be things you miss out here. What is it that you miss most?

Mark: I don't think we miss too much. During the growing season we're too busy. And we have an arrangement with one of our customers. They stay in Warsaw in December and January to enjoy real winters and we can use their apartment. We pay them in chickens, which works actually much better than using the official currency. In fact, more than fifty per cent of our business is based on direct trade. The Climate Tax on meat is a real pain in the ass for businesses like us.

So we spend long weekends in the city. First of all, our children can meet certain professionals to learn specific skills, e.g. native speakers for foreign languages. Then, of course, we visit musea and go to concerts. Moreover, we sometimes give courses to city people on growing vegetables. Some twenty years ago there was this interest in urban farming, which after a few years stopped. These days it is picking up again, people have a need for connecting to the physical world. Basically this has always been an underground current, but now it surges more than ever.

FU: Do you think your children would want to live here or in the city?

Mark: What not ask? Let's see who's around... Ah, there is Fiona, she is fourteen and our oldest child. Today she has been taking care of a group of toddlers.

Fiona: I am planning to live in the city in a few years time because there is no other option. I play the oboe and I want to become a professional musician. However, I already know I cannot stand to live in an apartment building. Thus, finding an appropriate spot to live is going to be challenge. And afterwards, I will return here. There are many benefits, such as living with our animals, being free of camera monitor, and I reckon there will still be disconnected spots to relax.

Lucas Janssen has experience in most of the disciplines related to the field of integrated water management. Currently he is with Deltares, a research and technology organization. Lucas lives in Wageningen, the Netherlands, near the river Rhine.

Fourteen

Offshore, a deep subsea well to sink

Todd Jarvis

> Water, water everywhere
> Nor any drop to drink
> Water, water everywhere
> Look offshore, a deep subsea well to sink

Apologies to *The Rime of the Ancient Mariner* by English poet Samuel Coleridge, but this passage is a fitting introduction to the future of water supplies as our Earth "ship" slips into uncharted waters in the wake of climate change. Yes, desalination of sea and brackish waters will likely become ever more popular as the costs per cubic meter continue to decrease. But the real opportunity is not the sea, per se, but rather what lies below the sea.

Researchers located on the driest continent, Australia, posit that 500,000 km^3 of freshwater are stored in subsea aquifers on continental shelves around the world. "The volume of this water resource is a hundred times greater than the amount we've extracted from the Earth's sub-surface in the past century since 1900." While the Australians are famous for hosting some of the most famous water diviners in the world, this discovery is not wishful thinking, but rather the result of careful examination of offshore drilling data for oil and gas on the continental shelves across the globe.

With so much water at our disposal as we spin towards Life Plus 2 Meters (and perhaps then some), why would there be any future talk of water wars? This is where things get deep as the legal arguments for who has access and ownership for sub-seabed water is not crystal clear. Does "groundwater" fall under the UN Commission on the Law of the Sea where countries can claim ownership to an Exclusive Economic Zone that extends 370 km offshore from its coastal baseline? Or is it possible that a variant such as the Law of the Hidden Sea might apply to deep groundwater that is hydraulically connected to the sea? Perhaps water stored in "fossil aquifers" such as offshore aquifers should be viewed as part of the common(s) heritage of humans? Or, perhaps government should step aside and let business into the world of groundwater governance much like how the US and Mexico are dealing with subsea hydrocarbons in the Gulf of Mexico by "unitizing" maritime transboundary reservoirs?

The underwater village of Atlit-Yam located offshore of Israel provides evidence that there is Life afterplus 2 Meters. The water supply of the village of Atlit Yam was apparently based in part on groundwater. One of the oldest wells in the world, a 7,500-year-old water well, lies between 8 to 12 meters beneath sea level in the Bay of Atlit.

Samuel Coleridge once said "Common sense in an uncommon degree is what the world calls wisdom." While climate change may be the "albatross around one's neck", the "commons" sense development of offshore aquifers will ultimately lead to more cooperation and wiser use of onshore water resources.

Todd Jarvis is a hydrogeologist with over 30 years of academic and industry experience. He blogs on water at Rainbow Water Coalition and wrote Contesting Hidden Waters: Conflict Resolution for Groundwater and Aquifers.

Tides will tear us apart 15

Emma J. Myatt

Dear Denise,

Congratulations! I cannot believe that by the time you get this, Zane will be fourteen weeks old. I wish there was a way to get news faster — how I miss the internet. I bet you're an amazing mother. I bet you're like Mum with a twist, a bit more craziness, a little less planned. You didn't say much about the birth — not sure how the hospitals are with you but here everyone's struggling a bit — (we now only get stories in the round-up papers at the end of the week in each town) and I've heard about a lack of drugs/pain relief and a total shortage of midwives.

It pisses me off that everyone saw all of this coming, and did nothing. But you know all this, no point in me ranting any more.

I want to meet Zane more than anything in the whole world. I am saving like mad but it'll still take me years — breaks my heart to think of missing all these early months. I'll keep doing the lotto — keep everything crossed.

Jake and I are okay. The kids are fine, working hard and hoping to get into the science projects over in the Highlands. There's been a massive investment in the projects lately and apparently the buildings are huge towering things that you can see for miles. I've not been up there, just too much to do here, but I've seen pictures. Leo is still good at maths and chemistry, and Lexi's a physics whizz. God knows where they get it from — not me, as you know — and Jake's still as into farming and solid earthy stuff as he ever was. I hope they get there. It's probably the only future I trust at the moment.

We hear stories from Aus, the ships bring papers and news but I dunno how much can be trusted and anyway, by the time they get here everything's six weeks old. I hear it's still hot, you are still getting plagues of insects and the fires are nuts, but at least you're getting more rain than before. I so hope I can see it for myself one day. The latest fares are around £17,500 per person. Jake and I can pull in about half this from anything we need to sell in a good quarter, but it goes, like a finger click, to pay for life and food and everything. We're stuck, really: if we grew our own we'd survive and not need to buy but then we'd have no money at all. Despite this I've managed to save. I've £2,000 in the bank, roughly. Jake's got some stashed in in the farm somewhere (he won't even tell me in case I let it slip to the gangs) but realistically it'll be years before we make it.

I miss you so much. Life here's good in many ways; we're still healthy and the kids can still learn. Our part of Scotland was pretty empty before as you know so the vanishing land hasn't had too much impact as yet. But however lucky we feel compared to some, I will never ever forgive myself for not coming with you when the fares were reasonable. I should have listened to Mum. I'll not go there, I go there every letter and it does me no good.

Has Zane got your eyes? Is he cheeky, like you were? Does he look like his auntie Lynn at all? I bet you'll be a great mum Denny.

You asked about the house. It's still here. The water's about three metres from the door at the highest tides. Last time I wrote it was four, so the rising's happening quicker than they all said. Nobody will buy it but, amazingly, the government has been good at making flood defences. We're getting insane storms and the house just gets engulfed by waves. We'd have washed away by now if not for the New Walls they've given us. Basically they're like huge sheets of plastic that have been put up all around the house — we've had them about two months now (did I write that we were getting them last time?) They got dug into what was the garden at low tide and they're higher than the roof. They're clear, so we can see through, but it's still like living in a goldfish bowl. If the house goes, we do get compensation but I don't dare tell you how much — it's practically nothing. No point moving until it goes, so we've stored all the important stuff in the high field in the barn, and the rest is stuff we can live without. The New Walls have doors, all water tight of course, and at high tide we can't enter or leave. It's so, so strange. Dad would have hated it and I'm so glad he's not here. Mum saw a little before she went to the home, but she's not seen it like this. She'd be heartbroken about the garden so we just don't tell her or show her pictures.

She's not doing too well actually Den. I don't know how much longer she'll be here. I'm glad you got to say goodbye properly. She has no regrets, just tells me to tell you that you did the right thing. And you did. All that space you have in Australia whilst we huddle on a shrinking rock, climbing higher with every tide, losing more land every week. Estimates say we've lost a tenth of the habitable land in the UK. It feels like more.

But we try to stay happy. I sound upbeat, I know. It's a habit I've got into for the kids' sakes, and it's hard to stop it.

The truth is though, we're terrified, Denny. Every day I wake up expecting to be wet. The sea's come faster than they said. It seems like a dream now when I think of how it was. Every morning I look outside through the weird New Walls and see the world, whitened through sea spray, the farm a little smaller. If the house goes we'll be moved to one of the new settlements over at Cairn o' Mount. They're like council estates from the early 2020s — remember the ones they built during the first housing crisis? Tiny ugly practical things with hardly any space per family. They're free, that's about the only bonus. We'll get allocated one as soon as we become homeless.

Maybe the rising will stop. After all, the ice has all gone, the travel rules have prevented any further air pollution. The limit on electricity will help, as will all the chem bans. But I feel it's all too late. Like I said, we knew this was coming. Remember the conversations we used to have about 'doomsday'? There was a guy in the papers last week saying how he felt doomsday had already come — that day when the damage done was too bad to reverse, whatever legislation we make now. I think he's probably right but we've got to hope, right?

I'll have to go. I can feel myself getting down and I don't want to do that... in the end I'll just end up telling you how shit it all is, and how we're all doomed here and I'll say again how short sighted I was not to come with you. See? I'm off already. I'll have to go and get this to the delivery office so it'll catch the boat on the 12th. I'll see it all the way, in a bag, making its way to you across all those massive oceans.

Anyway, I'm not down all the time. We keep upbeat. We can still buy whisky, when the tide's out it's almost like old times. Ha — do you remember when the garden first got a bit soggy and we thought it was the extra rain or a diverted spring? Then that wave, that just kept on coming? I often think of those early days, when you were still here, when it was all still media hype. I often try to call backwards in time down the years to younger versions of ourselves, to tell them to do something. Nobody would have listened, though. Everyone thought they were just crazy anarchists... crazy people who wanted to cause chaos... remember Paula, and how she stomped off to London with all those petitions? Most of what she wished for has, by necessity, been banned.

I miss all of it.

I want the world back.

I want my sister back. Come home... No, don't ever come home, it's not good here and it's going to get worse. The amount of people and the amount of Hill Houses just doesn't add up. I hope I'm dead by that time.

I said I wasn't going to get sad. I'm sorry Den.

I love you, and I love my new nephew, and I'll keep lotting and get the rest of us on that boat and come and join you. I can see your farm in my mind's eye. All that space.

Give Zane a big kiss for me, little sis.

XXXXXX
Lynn.

Emma J. Myatt is a full-time writer, full-time mother, chicken keeper and tutor who also runs a holiday let/writers' retreat. She writes in every scrap of spare time she can find and has been published on line in various places and in several anthologies.

# Sixteen

Two meters of migration

Binayak Das

Aminul stares at the vast land, no water, no rivers, and no boats. This is unlike his home of water and water. He has just landed in a resettlement colony stretching across arid land. He is a migrant, pushed away from his home on the southern fringes of Bangladesh by the encroaching sea. Aminul is not alone, thousands of people have turned climate migrants over the last five years. He is in Kazakhstan, a land he has never heard of.

He is in Kazakhstan because the 9th largest country in the world opened its borders, allowing climate migrants to join its 20 million citizens. Some of Bangladesh's 130 millions saw the need to leave their disappearing land for a safer and less-crowded space. Bangladesh's population density of 1,120 people per km^2 is far greater than Kazakhstan's 6 people per km^2. Kazakhstan welcomed those who could support its growing agricultural and energy sectors.

Aminul's journey was quick. His degree and knowledge of the gas industry made it easy to get a visa and job.

Others were not so lucky.

Shahid, a fisherman from the Chittagong region, was also suffering climate change pangs. He didn't have education, so he had to fight his way to higher elevations. Aminul flew to Kazakhstan in a day. Shahid turned to the trafficking networks set up 20 years earlier (during the Syrian war), trudging via boat, foot, and bus for two years to Kazakhstan.

Kazakhstan's new residents escaped the first threat of climate change, but Kazakhstan didn't open its gates willingly. With the onslaught of climate change submerging low-lying countries and small islands, people tried to escape by any possible means. Voices across the globe screamed for measures to avoid catastrophe. Europe, China, India and the US worried that their densely populated countries would be overwhelmed. Other countries with conflict, economic and political migrants said they could take no more.

Under pressure from all sides, the UN launched negotiations 10 years ago to cope with climate crisis migrants. Many proposals were put forward, but most were denied by "already burdened" countries. There was a risk that migrants without options would turn borders into bloodbaths.

And then came a shocking proposal from a tiny Pacific island: "land rich" countries such as Russia, Canada, Australia, and Kazakhstan could open their borders.

The first reactions from these countries was a big NO, but global and local protests made politicians reconsider. Trade-offs started to emerge as businesses and governments looked at migrants as a boon to their ailing economies and falling fertilities. Soon, they were joined by other countries seeking to combine labour and capital.

Within five years, people were moving ahead of climate change. Now Aminul and Sahidul stand, staring at a vast land without water, rivers and boats, looking to a different future.

And then they understood the second threat of climate change.

Binayak Das has about 16 years experience working on water, environment, climate change and sustainable development. He is currently associated with the Water Integrity Network in Berlin.

The Century of Division 17

Joe Cotton

STUDY NOTES: On the global crisis of climate and the Shikastan young (from *History of Shikasta* vol 3016: "The Century of Division")

I want to encourage a healthy amount of scepticism in you, dear student, with regard to the designation of the 21st Century as the "Century of Division", for you might rightly note that the great majority of Shikastan history was taken up by warring and conflict. Many argue (Taufiq among them) that it was in the Shikastans very nature to be hostile and aggressive, particularly towards those outside of their interactive group. Hence one could say the whole history of Shikasta was one of division! But I want to draw your attention to a more nuanced understanding of this designation by the Archivists. Shikastans were a fickle sort and an enemy of one decade could become the strongest of allies in the next. These shifting allegiances suggested that divisions could always be overcome — if only by the creation of another division in the form of a new common enemy. The global crisis of climate, however, was unique in that rather than being resolvable through new division, what was required was a unification on a scale unprecedented in Shikastan history. Yet as you know, rather than uniting in the spirit of international solidarity (which you may know as Envoy Johor's *Sense-of-We Feeling*), the Shikastans turned inwards to their own national groups, reinforced their borders, and forsook the rest of their kind. Consider the prophetic insights provided by Johor regarding the younger generation at the time:

> "... the young are, in their hordes, their gangs, their groups, their cults, their political parties, their sects, shouting slogans, in-

finitely divided, antagonistic to each other, always in the right, jostling for command. There they are — the future, and it is self-condemned" —Lessing (1981, 221).

Johor's description of the Shikastan young is key to understanding the "Century of Division". We can roughly categorise the young into two groups; *apathetics* and *radicals*, whereby the former were so disillusioned and lethargic as to renounce politics altogether, and the latter were effectively zealots of a particular ideology. Both groups, either through pessimism or narrow-mindedness, were quite unable to entertain the possibility that political divisions could ever be overcome. As the century progressed the radicals waged their ideological war, at first with words that increasingly took a parochial and nativist tone. Meanwhile the apathetics stood by — you may be familiar with the Shikastan saying that "the only thing necessary for the triumph of evil is for good [wo]men to do nothing" — the apathetics were, in their entirety, guilty of this. As the vitriol intensified, so international divisions between populations became insurmountable, and hateful words led to hateful deeds. It was this division that precluded an international resolution to the global crisis of climate, which in turn led the Shikastans to their end in the following "Century of Extinction". Johor observed the sorry occasion:

"The armies covered Shikasta. Meanwhile, the epidemics spread, among people, and among what was left of the animal population, among plant life. Meanwhile, the millions began to dwindle under the assault of famine. Meanwhile, the waters and the air filled with poisons and miasmas, and there was no place anywhere that was safe. Meanwhile, all kinds of imbalances created by their own manic hubris, caused every sort of natural disaster" —Lessing (1981, 296).

STUDY POINT: You should notice that in both excepts, Johor describes the Shikastans' problems as self-inflicted: they were "self-condemned... by their own manic hubris". Reflect on this observation with reference to the "Century of Destruction" (characterised by the two intensive periods of global conflict), the "Century of Division" (characterised by the collapse of international structures) and the "Century of Extinction" (characterised by the effects of the Global Crisis of Climate).

Remember: Following the extinction of the Shikastan population and the rebalancing of natural cycles, the colonisation of Shikasta shall begin anew. Be sure to emphasise lessons from Shikastan history that can inform future policies, so that previous mistakes can be learned from and our colonial effort might be more successful the second time around.

Joe Cotton, a recent graduate of Leiden University College, wrote this in the tradition of Doris Lessing's Shikasta. He is interested in politics, sustainability, philosophy, social justice, community engagement, education and climate change.

Eighteen

Manage better, now

Ralph Pentland

At the outset, I would like to point out that my own background is in water and environmental management. I do not profess to be an expert on climate — so my few remarks will be based as much on intuition as on science.

Let's begin with the basics — assuming the climate forecasters are somewhere near the right ballpark, the hydrologic effects of climate change could include changes in annual, seasonal and extreme precipitation, evaporation and runoff. There could also be an earlier onset of soil drying in early summer, and decreases in soil moisture availability. And in a cold climate like ours in Canada, we could experience a decrease in the ratio of snowmelt to rain, and an increase in the rate of snowmelt in spring months.

These hydrologic changes would translate into a number of water resources effects — for example, effects on drought and flood magnitude and frequency; supply reliability; demand requirements; and water quality and ecosystem habitat conditions.

Since water tends to be both an environmental and an economic integrator, these effects would affect a broad range of socio-economic activities — agriculture, forestry, hydroelectricity, industry, municipalities, recreation, shipping, and so on.

It seems to me the first step in preparing for climate change should be in identifying the areas and activities that are likely to experience the most serious negative impacts of an increasing greenhouse effect. Areas where water resources are already sensitive to climatic variability will probably be most vulnerable to the impacts of future climate change. Generally speaking, such areas have few or many of the following characteristics: natural water deficits, high societal demands, high flood risk, dependency on reliable seasonal supply, sensitivity to lake levels, decreasing water quality, dependency on hydroelectricity, and sensitive natural ecosystems.

Despite lingering predictive uncertainties, the implications for water resource systems are likely to include increased stress and more frequent failures. The apparent dilemma for water planners, managers and policy makers is whether to act on incomplete information, or to wait for more solid scientific support.

My own perception is that the dilemma is in fact more apparent than real, because the directions we should be moving to prepare for climate change are identical to those we should be moving anyway. Let me illustrate by way of a few examples:

- We should begin to seriously question the real viability and sustainability of proposed irrigation systems, and make the existing ones more water efficient, with or without climate change. Climate change may force us to do it sooner.

- We should discourage new development on flood plains and along susceptible shorelines, with or without climate change. Increasing climate variability may convince our citizens of the wisdom of that approach sooner.

- We should broaden our arsenal of weapons for combating water quality deterioration, with or without climate change. Climate change could induce us to do it sooner.

- We should price water and other environmental resources in such a way as to encourage their conservation — climate change may give us the incentive to do it sooner.

- We should do less subsidizing and more taxing of environmentally damaging activities, with or without climate change. Climate change could convince our lawmakers to do it sooner.

- Decentralized decision making, and application of user/polluter pays approaches should be practiced to the extent possible. These principles, which make sense anyway, are coming increasingly prudent with a less predictable future.

- Some claim that most countries have less water and environmental planning capability today than they had a few decades ago. To the extent that is correct, we should reverse that trend, with or without climate change.

Some have suggested massive capital works solutions — I disagree, with one small proviso. I would take climate change scenarios into account as a secondary design consideration for projects that we are building anyway. For example, it may be possible to design water management schemes, at little or no extra cost today, in such a way that they could be modified later, if necessary, in response to a changing climate.

I do not think we should even contemplate major capital works projects at this time just to deal with potential climate trends. For example, if it doesn't make economic sense now to further regulate the Great Lakes, we should not consider building capital works merely in anticipation of lower water supplies a few decades away — the evidence simply does not support it.

In fact, I would contend that the danger of over-reacting with structural measures is significantly greater than the danger of under-reacting. Let me elaborate by way of an admittedly far-fetched example. What would happen if two or more northern circum-polar countries were to decide simultaneously to solve their emerging drought problems by diverting some of their north-flowing rivers southwards?

Some oceanographers speculate that such an eventuality would affect arctic salinity gradients and climate circulation patterns in such a way as to actually accelerate the drying of the North American Great Plains. Whether one accepts that thesis or not, I am sure most would agree that the uncertainty alone is sufficient cause for caution.

In summary, what I am advocating is that we learn a lot more before contemplating any drastic adaptive measures, and that in the meantime, we simply do what we should be doing anyway — but that we do it much sooner and much better.

And cost should not be a serious concern. If my examples are anywhere near representative, a "sooner and better" strategy would almost surely result in long-term net savings.

Ralph Pentland served as Director of the Water Planning and Management Branch in Environment Canada from 1978 to 1991. Since 1991, he has served as a water and environmental policy consultant in many countries.

19
Bacon for everyone

Philip Ridgers

It was early September 2060, and the town of Flotsam was literally in hot water. Tom Williams wiped sweat from his sunburned brow, peered down the hill at a small boat meandering among pale chimneys and mosquito swarms.

'Poor folk,' he said, as the boat receded.

'Nothing to be done though,' said Dan, his brother. He'd had the sense to wear his black cap that morning.

'I suppose not,' Tom replied. 'Reckon they'll be back?'

Dan did not bother answering. The Styles family needed to find cows if they had a hope of returning. Most of Flotsam doubted anyone within a hundred miles had come across beef in ten years.

'Well good luck to them,' Tom said. He wrung sweat from his brown factory sleeve and wiped his face again. If it's this hot now, I dread midday. He thought the same thing every day.

'I s'pose we should get to work,' Dan said. 'Pigs don't kill themselves.'

They turned from the lake that had swallowed Bath a couple of decades earlier, and headed for the town slaughterhouse. Dan whistled as they walked.

'You're in a good mood,' Tom said. He watched his footing, careful not to tread in the copious amount of pig dung that covered much of the town.

'Well why not?' Dan asked.

'We just saw a family of four go to their likely deaths.'

'They've got a chance. The professors gave them a month's worth of insulin.'

'Pig insulin.'

Dan shrugged. 'It's all we've got. Better than nothing, right?'

Tell that to Anne Styles, Tom thought. All three of her boys had grown resistant to porcine insulin, and their blood sugars were constantly skyrocketing.

Flotsam was primarily diabetic. Some doctors with type one diabetes had made their home in an abandoned MOD site, on the hill of what had been Lansdown in Bath. As the waters rose, someone found it amusing to call the place Flotsam. The name had stuck. They made insulin for themselves from pig pancreases, and diabetics had rushed to the area.

'Maybe they'll manage to get some live beef after all,' Dan said. 'Dr Shortwick can have the pancreases, the rest of us can eat something different for once.'

'And the waters will recede, and everything will be fixed,' Tom said. 'We'll walk down to the city centre like we did thirty years ago, when we were kids. Maybe we'll even go for lunch at the Royal Crescent hotel cos we'll be rich too.'

'Sarcasm only buys you an injury,' Dan replied.

'All right, save that for the pigs,' Tom said. They pushed through the doors of a makeshift barn. It was even hotter inside, and the smell was incredible. Men and women were already hard at work, herding squealing pigs into a large room.

'Oi, Williams and Williams! You're late,' shouted Rick. The bald old man was in charge of butchery. Tom wondered why he bothered with a meat cleaver, his tongue could almost lash skin from bone.

'We were seeing off the Styles,' Dan said.

'Grab knives, and use 'em an extra hour past everyone else,' Rick said.

'Balls,' Dan said, though not loudly enough for Rick to hear. 'I want to get my Friday started on time.'

'It's only fair,' Tom replied, picking up a long sharp knife. He joined the other workers, waiting outside the room of pigs. Someone pulled a lever, and CO_2 stunned the squealing swine.

'They get a comfier death than most of us,' Dan said.

'That's cos the whole world's gone to the pigs,' Tom replied. 'But they should enjoy it while it lasts.' Like everything else, Flotsam was low on CO_2.

A gong sounded. The workers moved through the doors and among the unconscious swine. Tom grabbed the hind legs of an enormous sow, dragged it onto a table with Dan's help. He ran his knife across its throat, grimaced as blood poured copiously.

We need more aprons, he thought. He doubted his three minutes of authorised shower time would give him a chance to clean his clothes properly.

Soon, dead pigs were being hacked into their various useful parts. Dan started whistling again as he chopped.

'You know what tonight is,' he said.

'Obvious statement awards night?' Tom asked. It was the hour of power. Once a month, Flotsam's mayor allowed residents to draw an hour's worth of electricity from the grid for entertainment purposes.

'What shall we enjoy?' Dan asked.

'I was thinking a film,' Tom said. 'We could invite Bella and Amanda over.'

'It'll cost us,' Dan replied, chopping away. 'Bella's had three hypos this month. She's almost through her glucose rations already, and looking for help.'

'We'll just say no,' Tom said.

Dan laughed. 'When have you ever resisted her smile?'

Fair point, Tom thought. 'It'll be fine,' he said. 'I'll persuade her to see the docs, reduce her insulin dose. If she sits nice and still, she'll be ok. I'll do the cooking, serve up my world famous regulation bacon, sausage and cabbage.'

'You convinced me,' Dan said, his broad chest spattered red. 'We should watch that cartoon with the toys.'

'That's almost an hour and a half long.'

'We'll just act the first part of it then.'

Tom grimaced. 'Don't you dare...' he began, but it was too late.

Dan started singing the first words from the old cartoon...

I hate that bloody song, Tom thought. Dan sang it about six times a day. However, Tom seemed to be in the minority. To his horror, other workers started singing along.

In barbershop harmony.

'You've ruined it even more,' Tom said. 'When the hell did you find time to rehearse?'

'Oh come on, it's catchy,' Dan replied. Then, he launched into the chorus. Tom tried to frown, but a smile tugged at his mouth. He had to admit, they were rather good. He hummed along in spite of himself. Before long, everyone was singing.

The heat gathered, pig entrails were everywhere, and music covered the town of Flotsam.

Philip Ridgers is a piano teacher and accompanist currently living in Bath. When he's not busy at a piano, he also enjoys writing. As a type 1 diabetic, it was a natural choice for him to centre his contribution around diabetes.

Twenty

Passports or people? Choose one.

David Zetland

The first passports were issues centuries ago, but it wasn't until after World War I that travelers needed them to cross borders, prove their identity, and protect their rights as citizens, both domestically and abroad.

Passports allowed their holders to pass through the ports (gates) of diplomatic and bureaucratic walls. People without passports could not pass from their original country to another country. (Illegal crossings could only go so far before they were prevented.)

Passports are valuable precisely because they separate humans into two groups: those who may pass, and those who may not.

In many cases, people do not worry about this difference because they do not care to leave their countries of origin, but there are numerous examples of people taking dramatic risks or paying exorbitant sums when they want to leave their countries but lack the proper paperwork.

Migrants face costs of all kinds. They leave behind their families, friends, and place in the world. They are willing to bear those costs because they think the benefits of their new home to be worthwhile.

The cost of moving has increased as passport (and visa) requirements have tightened over the past century. During World War I, refugees could flee violence for safer places. During the 1920s and later, they were trapped behind bureaucratic walls that could not be breeched without the right papers.

The entire plot of the 1942 movie, "Casablanca," depends on the heroes getting the right visa, but the movie's happy ending was denied to the millions of refugees and political prisoners (most famously, the Jews) who died through government action or neglect. The situation is not much different today for the people who want to flee cruel and deadly places (North Korea, Eritrea, Syria, etc.) but lack papers.

Some people might think that the suffering of would-be migrants is a price worth paying to protect their own homes from being overrun and pockets emptied to help refugees, but those people (usually members of the lucky sperm club born with the right papers) miss the obvious middle option of allowing migration without the gold-plated protections they expect themselves. Most migrants are less interested in handouts than in safety and the opportunity to work and contribute to their adoptive communities.

Passports will become more valuable in a climate-changed world as disruptions (failed crops, miserable weather, sinking cities, violence, etc.) increase the value of moving. Refugees — human and animal — will seek to cross borders as their domestic prospects deteriorate. Some of these refugees will have more money (those fleeing record temperatures in the Persian Gulf or abandoning beachfront houses on tropical islands), but most refugees will be the poor who cannot feed or protect themselves.

The increased importance of passports will mean

that those with good passports will be very interested in ensuring their identity is protected. People with bad passports, on the other hand, will be willing to pay more to get forged passports (or obtain real passports via fraud). Those forces will complement each other in driving governments to increase the security of their passports.

A few months ago, I was extremely upset when I opened the washing machine to find my passport. We were leaving to South America in a week, and there was no time to get a replacement, so I took a chance. Luckily, the damage was too small to affect the passport's function, but I really thought a lot about how vulnerable I was without that document and the rights it gave me. No border guard, soldier or police officer is interested in my charm, blog or business card. The only thing that stood between me and deportation was a 32-page booklet.

Passport controls and identity are going to get very important, very quickly if even half the predictions of climate change come to pass. To me, that implies that we are going to replace passports with technology that's harder to forge or lose, such as implanted RFC chips, tattoos (yes, I'm saying it), DNA-registration, and other technologies that can pass through the wash without losing their validity.

Is this inevitable? Not exactly. Passports were put into widespread use over 100 years ago at the behest of governments that wanted to control who went where. The balance of costs and benefits has kept that system in place, but that balance could tip entirely over if enough pressure is applied. The arrival of numerous undocumented aliens in the US and EU (and China's breaking documentation system) suggests that controls are fragile, just as the rise of digital currencies (and continuing attraction of gold) has shown people's mistrust of government motives.

In the future, we may all need to scan ourselves to the authorities on a daily basis, to prove that we have the right to be where we are — or we may just need to find ways to live among a variety of people.

Will we value humans or paperwork? If your answer depends on what passport you're holding right now, then I suggest you imagine how you'd answer if that passport was gone.

David Zetland is an assistant professor at Leiden University College, where he teaches various classes on economics. He blogs on water, economics and politics at `aguanomics.com` *and founded the "Life Plus 2 Meters" project.*

Slowly too late

Majel Haugh

Slowly
The light enters our eyes
Slowly
The answers now too late
Lie scattered on university tables
In books
In speeches
In films
Plans are hurriedly hatched
To save what is left
Too slow
Too late

Majel Haugh is a writer based in Limerick city. Her work has appeared in Abridged, Limerick Literary Revival and Burning Bush 2.

Twenty-two

The beach that ate Silicon Valley

Jennifer LaForce

Silicon Valley, California. You can admire it; you can hate it. Most of the world's leading edge technology either comes from here or is made usable here. Tucked into the northern reaches of the San Francisco Bay, you will find an old quay in the tiny towns of Alviso and Milpitas. Here the bay is shallow: 85 percent of the water is less than 30 feet deep. Circulation depends on strong tidal action, river inflow, winds and storms. From a wildlife perspective, the salt marshes are highly productive and very valuable. When the tide is high, many fish species forage for food along the shore. Once the tide goes out, water birds feast on those unfortunate enough to get stuck.

    Not too long ago, the Milpitas quay was a destination. Standing on the old pilings, a little imagination takes you on Sunday boat rides in 1915 or even farther back to a Native American fishing for dinner.

Now there is a new kind of production on the quay. Not quite sky scrapers, new commercial buildings full of valuable equipment and more valuable ideas indicate that the recession is over and Silicon Valley is pushing at the edges of its geography yet again. Water treatment plants responsible for most of the usable water in the Bay area dot the marsh shores. Highway 237 is a critical connection between continental California and the San Francisco peninsula, connecting the states two major highways, 880 along the eastern side of the bay and 101 along the western side.

A sea-level rise of 2 meters has all of Milpitas and Alviso completely underwater. Highway 237 will belong to the sea creatures as will much of Highway 101.

Such a sea-level rise will inundate both developed and natural areas, cause salinity contamination of groundwater aquifers and rivers, damage ports and recreational beaches. The cost of protecting against sea-level rise is large, but often below the value of the property protected. Preventative ("Hey! Don't build there!") and/or defensive actions taken today can prevent large damages in the future

Numerous studies have been done and there is no need to reproduce their conclusions. What is strangely remarkable about the rise in sea-level and the corresponding results is how we, as California communities, respond to it in almost exactly the same way we respond to homelessness.

If you don't know by now that it costs less to house a homeless person than to leave them on the streets, you just don't want to know. Between jail time and emergency room visits, it costs about $30,000 a year for a homeless person to be on the streets. Add business loss, shelter costs and the figure increases to a staggering $40,000 a year. Guess what, they could be in a home for a lot less.

Since costs are spread across many individuals, it is hard for any one person to recognize or respond to these facts.

Likewise the value of property threatened by sea-level rise in Silicon Valley is extremely high because of past development and getting higher every day because of new development. Around the perimeter of the Bay, existing commercial, residential, and industrial structures threatened by a two-meter sea-level rise is valued at $100 billion.

Perhaps because of the slow rate of increase of sea level or perhaps because the individual can't see it, there is little advanced planning and an inadequate response to these facts.

I've worked in disabled and disadvantaged communities for 30 years. I understand emotional response. I understand bias. But I have yet to figure out why my peers cannot step beyond both when presented with indisputable fact. If we could figure this out, we could address the fact that the sea level is rising without over or under reacting. We could address homelessness and probably every other polarizing issue. For me, that's the task to undertake.

Jennifer LaForce is a Business Consultant in Silicon Valley, missionary, author and traveler with the grandiose goal of understanding why we do what we do.

23
I don't like these storms anymore

Ben Ruddell

As a kid in the Midwest, the distant rolling thunder of a summer soaker was soothing, and the lightning bolts were exciting, bursting with neon light and color. Those storms were beautiful, with their sunbursts, whipping winds, and towering black clouds sweeping across the flat open land.

Those storms changed, flooding fields and towns but leaving withered crops and dry riverbeds in the summer. Those tenacious farm towns survived fifty years of depopulation, but collapsed as the groundwater ran out and the corn moved north to Canada. We followed so many others when fled the economic blight of the Midwest for greener pastures in the Mountain West. There were jobs, and the reservoirs had enough water for the dry spells.

The Southwest was so beautiful: pristine pine forests ringing towering mountains, vistas and red rocks, deserts and flowers. I never saw anything like it, and once I came I never wanted to leave. We had storms here, too, but they brought the most welcome rain to the arid hills. And rainbows — so many rainbows in these desert storms. No wonder these mountain towns are so popular. Everyone wanted to come here.

The kids felt the fear before I did. We tried to calm them when the lightning struck, but they felt a fear too deep for a parent to reach, a fear I didn't understand. My oldest piled rocks around a tree to keep it safe from the lightning. It was cute. I thought he would grow out of it, but he didn't; we did. Us older folks fooled ourselves with a lifetime of false experience.

When I first smelled the smoke, I felt that same fear — ominous, imminent, unavoidable. The fires were all over the summer news. A million acres here, a hundred houses there, year after year. Fort McMurray burned in Canada, but it was always far away. Still, my subconscious mind was catching on. The lightning made me jumpy, and if nobody was looking I would walk nervously to the window to check for smoke. I wrote my Congressmen about funding for the Forest Service after I read they only had money to manage a tiny fraction of the public forest in these mountains.

Every year the fires were worse than the last, and Congress finally funded the overdue thinning project out here. It was ten years of work, billions of dollars. It was too late for us. That big, dry monsoon storm came in at the wrong time, and the lightning set the forest ablaze in a thousand fires. A hundred years of overgrown fuel went up in smoke, along with the power transmission lines and half of the town. It was all the fire service could do just to keep the highway open for evacuation.

The fires left a charred and sediment-choked moonscape. The power and water were out for a long time, and most of us had nothing to come back to after the evacuation. The tourists and students vanished, and with them my job. We moved back east to live with family, and figured out how to make ends meet. We survived, but things aren't the same. I heard that a few of the mountain towns are recovering, but only rich vacationers can live there now. These fires woke middle class folks like us from our Southwestern dream.

Now, on those the terribly hot Chicago summer nights when the rain falls, I tell the kids these storms are as beautiful as I remember from my childhood, and we're lucky to be here. But to tell the truth, I don't like these storms anymore.

Ben Ruddell is from the Midwestern U.S. and lives in Flagstaff, Arizona with his wife Jennifer and their children. This vision is vaguely autobiographical.

Twenty-four

A village's uncertain future

Tran Thi Kim Lien

In one study in my hometown — a mountainous area in North Central Region of Vietnam, we considered Huong Lam commune — one of the vulnerable areas of climate change in Ha Tinh province. The commune is home to 6,673 people in 1,636 households with an average population density of 400 people/km^2. Their main livelihood activities are agriculture, small industries, trades and services. Our study found that this commune faces risk from floods, droughts, cold and storms.

The most immediate impact of drought is a reduction and even loss in crop production (paddy rice, peanut, maize, etc.) due to inadequate and poorly distributed rainfall. Another severe impact of droughts is water shortages. Lower pasture production from droughts may also decrease fodder supplies. With little land available, the people cannot reduce risk through diversification. The unusual dry conditions since the end of 2015 (allied with El Niño) have led to severe droughts around the country.

The worst agricultural losses are from floods that arrive with typhoons. Floods destroy both standing crops (paddy rice and fruit trees) and stored food. They also increase fungal infections that destroy seeds for the next planting. Floods of 2–3 days cause serious health problems for people (in particular, the disabled and elderly) who live in poor conditions with limited food sources, polluted water sources, and poor sanitation.

The Vietnam Ministry of Natural Resources and Environment projects that medium emissions climate change scenarios (B2) will increase annual rainfall by 2-7 percent by 2100, with less rain in the dry season and more in the rainy season. Maximum daily rainfall may double in the North Central zones (including in Ha Tinh). Typhoons can uproot crops, damage trees, and destroy housing and animal shelters. Climate change will change the intensity, frequency and (un)predictability of storms. In Ha Tinh, storms that normally occur from August to October are sometimes showing up in April, causing greater damage due to their unpredictable frequency and intensity.

The people of Huong Lam will not find it easy to adapt.

Tran Thi Kim Lien holds Bachelors and Masters degrees in Forest Science and Management from Vietnam and Australia, respectively. She now focuses on helping local people understand their vulnerabilities and adapt to climate change.

The sentencing 25

Annie Percik

"Life plus two metres!"

A collective gasp travels around the courtroom, and the judge's gavel comes down like the final nail in my coffin.

I hear the words but I can't process them. There are fingers clutching painfully at my arm, and I look down into the despairing eyes of my mother.

"We'll fight this," she says, trying to sound confident, but failing by several degrees.

The likelihood that any appeal will go through before the worst part of the sentence is carried out is vanishingly small. And, once that part is done, there's no going back, no matter what may be decided later.

I'm still finding it difficult to understand what's going on. I realise I've stopped breathing, and I force myself to take in a strained lungful of air. Suddenly, my knees feel weak and I slump down onto the wooden bench, utterly defeated.

For a crime I didn't commit, I have been given the heaviest sentence possible. I will have to serve a lifetime of indentured servitude, working the hardest tasks in the most inhospitable and dangerous environments. It's no consolation that the other part of my sentence will equip me better for such work than I am now. It is not an equipping I want or will be able to endure without great suffering.

Sooner than I can imagine at this moment, I will be taken from this place and delivered to the Department of Transmogrification. There, my bones will be broken and extended, and my body stretched almost beyond its capacity, adding a full two metres to my height. Then, I will be provided with acclimatisation training, to teach me how to live and move in my new body, and how to use it to the benefit of the establishment that has forced it upon me.

I have heard tell that everything slows down when the two metres are added. Having such reach and such mass may be useful in undertaking certain types of manual labour and military tasks, but it necessarily results in a slowing of all movements and accompanying thought processes. It is not possible to utilise the familiar speed and flexibility of the human body on a grander scale.

I will no longer be able to meet the gaze of my friends and family eye to eye, even if I get the opportunity to see them at all. I will no longer even be able to relate to them on a level playing field. They will never be able to comprehend my new existence, and I will quickly forget what it is like to be one of the small and hasty beings that will soon be scurrying beneath my notice.

It may be a life sentence, but it will be the end of the life I have known up until now. The person I am now will cease to exist as surely as if I was to be executed. A new being will take up my newly assigned role in society, with different abilities, a different perspective, and different companions in my servitude.

My mind shies away from the implications of what has just happened, and I retreat into the oblivion of unconsciousness, hoping I will awake to discover it has all been a dream. More likely, I will awake to a nightmare of a new existence I will have to endure for the rest of my life.

Annie Percik lives in London with her husband, Dave, where she is revising her first novel. She also publishes a photo-story blog recording the adventures of her teddy bear. He is much more popular online than she is.

Twenty-six

Coastal freshwater aquifers join the sea

Nazli Koseoglu

Global sea level is rising at an accelerating rate in response to global warming. As temperatures increase, ice growth in winter falls behind ice melt in summer resulting shrinkage of nearly all surveyed glaciers worldwide. According to the U.S. Environmental Protection Agency, decline in ice cover increases amount of freshwater lost to the oceans and has already added about eight inches to the average sea level since Industrial Revolution. The IPCC forecasts continuation of this trend in increasing sea levels over the course of this century with 0.4 to 0.8 metre additional rise as a result of historical emissions even if the zero emissions are achieved.

On the other hand a more pessimistic, or realistic, scenario by the World Bank predicts up to 2 metres increase in the sea level assuming global carbon emissions remain unabated. A 2-metre rise in sea levels means an extreme reshaping of coastlines, possible flooding of many low-lying and coastal cities, and severe inundation of several islands. Next to the well-documented concern for coastal and lowland flooding risk, another yet under-reported impact of sea level rise will be on the freshwater systems. When the freshwater level drops lower than the equilibrium in coastal aquifers, saltwater with higher density, thus with higher pressure, is allowed further in land and salinize groundwater resources. This phenomenon is defined as salt intrusion. Moreover as the sea level goes up beyond tolerable, the interface between ground and seawater changes and intrusion risk increases, significantly impacting local drinking water availability of coastal communities. Basement and septic system failures and deterioration of marshland ecosystems fed by coastal aquifers are other further hazards of the sea level rise associated with coastal aquifers.

Climate-related hazards threaten human and environmental systems whose vulnerability will increase with greater exposure. There are wide variety of physical mitigation and social adaptation options of varying effectiveness that could be combined in dealing with reducing the pressure of sea level rise on the coastal aquifers. While physical measures are mainly barriers insulating and recharging aquifers or removing saltwater, social measures are more about adapting behaviour such as changing or limiting withdrawal patterns from coastal aquifers. However each measure requires a definite level expertise for implementation and comes at a certain capital, operation or opportunity cost to communities at risk that are not always able to afford them. This adds up to the immense external costs and injustices of global warming that we do not account for.

Multiple factors affect the vulnerability to salt intrusion in coastal aquifers of different geological characteristics at different altitudes, and sea level-groundwater dynamics has a high level of inherit uncertainty due to these complexities. The occasional mismatches in sea level rises at local and global scale also contribute to the challenge of determining a rule of thumb indicator or transferable decision support tool to assess vulnerability to sea level rise and type of mitigation measure fit for different cases.

Nazli Koseoglu is a PhD student from the School of Geosciences, University of Edinburgh, UK. Her PhD looks into the valuation and optimization of water use in Scotland to increase social return from freshwater resources.

A view from dry land 27

Clay Reynolds

Growing up on the semi-arid prairies of West Texas, I didn't care much about sea-levels. As a boy, I never saw a river I couldn't walk across, although becoming stuck in quicksand or victimized by some random vermin or other while breaking through the wild-plum thickets along the sandy banks of our neighborhood creek and riverbeds was a threat. When I first saw the Mississippi, I couldn't believe it. These times of my childhood where I grew up were the years of drought. It lasted seven years, actually, so oceanic waters meant little to me. Although as an infant my family visited California and, I was told, spent time on the beach, I have no memory of the Pacific. I didn't even see the Gulf of Mexico until I was twelve, and the Atlantic wasn't in my experience for another decade.

So the whole idea of rising ocean levels is hard for me to imagine, even now, and even after I've lived on the coast for ten years and been on ships at sea. I've walked the seawalls of major cities that border oceans, and I'm sensitive to the power of rising tides, but it's an intellectual rather than an emotional perception. I am still, I guess, emotionally on dry land.

Years ago I saw a documentary about divers exploring the drowned remains of some ancient city. The presumption was that an earthquake had opened the entire city to the bay that wrapped around it, submerging it suddenly and completely to a depth of twenty or thirty feet. The cameras showed divers swimming into and out of doorways and around columns of ancient, forgotten buildings, once home to an active and large population. The sensation of watching this film stayed with me. It was more than the ghostly exploration of a dead city, more than the speculation of what happened to the people who once walked these streets and lived in these sunken structures. It reminded me that Nature has little regard for the pitiful etchings of mankind. When Atlas, so to speak, more or less shifts his weight, just a little, the world shifts with it, and prairies buckle, mountains crumble, oceans rise.

The two-meter rise of the oceans forecast by the dark prophets of science is not something, though, to be casually regarded. Man's refusal to respect and preserve the planet/garden where he exists is the cause of this, they say and I believe. I have seen reports of soot-covered glaciers, of the diminished ice-packs in Greenland, Antarctica, the rapidly disappearing rain forests, and I've felt desperately sad, even a little bit afraid. I note that recently, a cruise ship traversed the previously impenetrable Northwest Passage, which, triumphant an achievement as that may be, signals a crisis with polar ice. I worry about that, and I worry about polar bears and penguins and whales and other creatures of the sea that rely on the stability of oceans to survive.

Water rising two meters doesn't sound like much. In American terms, that's a couple of yards. But the global impact of that on low-lying cities such as New York or San Francisco, Boston and Charleston, Miami and Mobile, and most certainly New Orleans and Corpus Christi would be horrific. And that's just in the U.S. In more than a minor way such a rise would remap the coastlines of all the continents. And while it might not sink entire cities, it could change their perimeters, force them to face ruination and disappearance of their most precious icons and landmarks.

The focus of the media when they deign to talk about this in serious terms is the economic impact, of course. Loss of property would be one — oceanfront is prime real estate almost anywhere — and certainly loss of business from shipping, fishing, and other seaside enterprises. Tourism would be affected; the famous beaches where people go to frolic and take the sun and surf would be altered in dynamic ways.

But apart from the grim and somewhat temporal

realities, there is the emotional impact of all of this. It's our fault. It's our problem to fix, and we do nothing about it, not really.

When I was a boy in my drought-stricken homeland, I remember that some people came "to town," which is how it was phrased, driving animal-drawn conveyances. Mules and horses pulled carriages and wagons into the wagon-park that was behind the main buildings of Main Street and across from the depot. I was five or six at the time, but it seemed perfectly normal to me. I understood that they weren't doing this to be quaint; this was their principal form of transportation. I'm not that old. This was only sixty years ago in rural West Texas. But we have moved from that to automobiles so entirely, I'd speculate that in that same county today, no more than a fraction of the population has ever ridden in, let alone driven, a mule or horse-drawn wagon. We've come that far.

As I sit here and compose this on an electronic machine, comfortably cooled by air conditioning, knowing that in a while, I'll fire up my vehicle and drive into the city where I will teach a class in a comfortably chilled classroom bathed in electric light and enhanced by electronic devices, I don't pause and marvel at the progress that has been made in the past six decades. But I do worry that maybe the price of that progress may be measured in meters, the measurement of the rise of the oceans.

I think there are two truths here: High tide is coming, and there is nothing we can do to stop it, as we lack the collective will to truly assess our carelessness and count the cost or to try, even, to reverse the slide toward submersion. And in time, I suspect, divers will be exploring the drowned ruins of our civilization. The question then, is if there will still be people high enough and dry enough to care.

Clay Reynolds has authored more than a thousand publications ranging from academic articles and essays to award-winning short fiction and novels. A native of Texas, he is Professor of Arts and Humanities at the University of Texas at Dallas.

Twenty-eight

A family farm in the future

Kai Olson-Sawyer

Bill Mattson, a Minnesota farm owner-operator, sent this letter to his children when he passed along the family farm.

September 6, 2052

Dear Liz, Dean and Mary,

 As I near retirement in my 74th year (not soon enough for you worrying about Dad's old bones), I wanted to offer a brief history of Mattson Acres Farm. Although you always laugh at me when I do it, I dusted off my trusty keyboard to give you a sense of the changes that have befallen our farm over the last 40 years. While I know that Dean is wavering on farming and Mary is off to other things, I want you all, not just Liz, to understand this land's past because it's also our family's past. You also know how much I love keeping records for posterity's sake (and to tell a good story).

It starts in 2011 when your mom and I were able to save the money to buy that parcel of Nordinger's land and make it our own after leasing it for years. Besides marrying your mom and witnessing your births, that was the proudest day of my life. Mom always said that Good Thunder was a good luck place to farm.

The first 451 acres was about split between corn and soybean. We were fairly profitable with the high commodity prices in the years before and after acquiring that land. Although prices softened later in the teens, the Big Dry really hurt.

I'm sure you all remember how stressful that time was with record-low rain and unbearable heat from 2021-2025. Those wilted fields left us just eking out an existence with terrible yields that put us in the red. Mom was wise to keep pushing us towards more crop insurance. We also decided to adjust our crop mix, which was our first step down that road.

We were hoping for rain, and eventually it arrived. Once that rain began to fall in February 2026, it never seemed to stop. At first the Big Wet was a boon and made up for the moisture loss and increased crop yields. That year was decent, but the problems were soon rising with the Cobb River. Never will I forget when the Cobb and Maple Rivers met on our land. In all, we saw a record 70 inches of rain in 2027. Over half of our crops were lost to flood and much of the rest succumbed to root rot and fungus.

The amount of water we saw on our land was staggering and something I never could have imagined. The nub of it is that we're lucky our farm survived. With insurance, your mom's job at the library and a little luck, we made it.

Water is always a problem, but we knew we had to act in a big way. After all those years of loading up our soil with fertilizers, baked in by the Big Dry, the torrential runoff from our fields picked up that pollution and put it right back into the rivers and groundwater. Good thing I've always been adamant about regularly testing our well water because in 2028 and 2029 the nitrate levels were sky high. If we weren't aware of those toxins and fortunate to afford that reverse osmosis filtration, who knows how badly we could've been sickened.

Between our fouled water and the erratic weather, we knew we had to act on what Charlie at extension services called "drought and deluge." Even though the weather is always changing, it was evident that we couldn't count on the past for any indication of the extreme weather or precipitation that could strike. Climate change was tearing us up and we decided we were going to fight back (and hard).

Despite uncertainty, we worked with extension to come up with a solid plan. At the time we bought our final thousand acres I'd been playing with different crop mixes. I made a commitment then to see it through. Corn, yellow pea, alfalfa, soy, lentil — I tried it all and more to varying success. Continuous tinkering with the mix and rotation of the crops became so integrated into the health and well-being of our crop yields, our soil's water and nutrient retention, and the farm's economic viability, that it's of the utmost importance to the farm's resilience. Not only does this fine-tuning concern our cash crops, but it turns out that finding the right mix for our cover crops is just as essential. The diversity of crops that we produce has enabled our farm to withstand the higher temperatures, pests and the whipsaw dry and wet times we experience. Our farm has worked with Mother Nature to adapt to whatever is thrown our way.

The other major strategy on our farm was taking the land out of production through buffers and the conservation easement in the early 2030s. It was a hard choice and a burden even with USDA grants, but preserving those 300 acres for wetlands helped clean up nitrate pollution from our water and our neighbors' water downstream. We had the foresight to head off the federal 2041 Green Waters Act and get a handle on our pollution numbers before we had to report them, and as you know, we've always beat the nutrient diet standards. It was heartening when the Garcia's joined our easement, which really started a trend around here. (We're trendsetters!) Opening that land to duck hunting with assistance from the Waterfowl Association has been a real economic win.

All I can say is that we've worked hard to sustain this farm now and into the future. To keep the farm going under constantly changing conditions, we need to watch, learn, act, repeat: It never ends. That's all we can do to deliver the best possible outcomes. I hope you keep farming to the end of the century.

Love always, Dad

Kai Olson-Sawyer is a writer and senior research and policy analyst for GRACE Communications Foundation.

29
The bore is coming

Sarah Dixon

The bore is coming.

It comes, as it always has, to its peak near the autumn equinox. Experts predict that, after a summer of incessant rainfall on top of already record water levels, it will be catastrophic. Catastrophic. This is not a word that has ever been applied to the Severn Bore in all the thousands of times man has watched water surge and roll along the river's course.

In years gone by it was a popular tourist attraction; people walked the banks and viewed the bore as it hissed and crashed its way upstream. It's been years since anyone dared stand on the banks; not that the banks are where they were before the water rose, or we sank, depending on your perspective.

My perspective is a hillside, across the valley from my retirement home. The house was once a pleasant rural retreat; In the sticks, as my wife used to say. In the arse end of nowhere, I would counter. We bought it to retire to. In our late 50's, good luck and good decisions left us still young enough to have our health, to be in love, and wealthy enough to enjoy our retirement.

At that time the ramshackle property, nestled in woodland several metres from the river bank, seemed an ideal place to spend our days. My wife wanted to set up a small business, growing Bonsai trees, and I was going to write the novel I'd been promising myself all these years. The kids were grown and on their own way. We had been good, responsible citizens for decades and now was the time to reap the rewards.

Then the water rose; not slowly as we'd thought but with alarming quickness. Remote sounding scientists were portending 'tipping point', the latest in a long line of terrifying prophecies that had failed to come true; AIDS, the Millennium Bug, Bird Flu, Zika... They shouted loud enough but the media had been using the tactics of hysteria to sell news for years. We were immune.

The Totten Iceberg in East Antarctica had never read the news, and it was indifferent to the reception its inevitable melting would receive; it didn't do it for attention, it did it because it was ice, and when ice gets warm enough, it melts.

Within weeks the water that had run, benignly brown along the floor of the valley below us swelled with the melt water from a broad strip to a swollen, hungry torrent. A vicious snake that had swallowed something large; distended, struggling, angry.

We sat on the balcony, where we had envisaged enjoying afternoon tea, or pre-dinner drinks in the summer evenings, and watched the water become a steady stream of bloated animal corpses; not all the farmers had higher ground to take their beasts too. The turgid, turbulent water snatched up anything in its path, the weight of it enough to pull trees from the earth or gather up buildings and send them, flotsam and jetsam, on their way. It was as if the Gods were playing poo sticks, my wife noted on the day before she left.

Don't worry, it isn't the end of our marriage. It was just the end of our time here; We had the official warning and knew that our house would likely be swept away with the next bore. Our insurance company stated their refusal to pay; we are at fault for not having the prescience to sell before we knew there would be a disaster, it seems. I don't know if we would have done that, even if we had known. This was our dream. If it is to sink without a trace, then we should watch it do so; the captain and his ship and all that. We couldn't have slept at night, if we'd sold on inevitable disaster in place of a dream.

We live with my son and his wife now, it's a squeeze but we get along. There's no space for Bonsai trees, no quiet for writing, but there is the joy of Grandchildren. You have to make the best of what you've got.

My wife didn't understand why I wanted to come and watch, she called it morbid. Her eyes brimmed with tears that only abated when I made the poor joke, 'Don't add to the water level, old girl.' She's at home.

I've found myself a spot, high and dry, sitting on a tree stump. I have a flask; the bitterly aromatic tea is clouding the air before me. The cup warms the chill in my hands but it doesn't touch the ice in my guts, or overwhelm the musky dampness of falling leaves and rotting timbers. They seem appropriate for today, not the day of the dead, but the day of dying dreams.

Somewhere, out in the wide ocean, a wave has formed; larger than they ever were, swollen with melt from good old Totten and not just the tip; the whole nine yards. The wave crashes angrily to shore, the force of it loosening cliffs, stealing shale. But there is a weak point, the estuary; here the water finds a place to run.

Imagine a funnel, loyally taking the water you pour in and directing it to a single point. Now imagine throwing a bucket full of water into the funnel; imagine the force that it sprays from the end.

The water throws itself, unknowing, unfeeling, into the Severn. The estuary roils. Near Avonmouth the swell is terrifying but it is just the beginning. The bore itself forms past Sharpness when the weight of the water hits the rocks at Hock Cliff. Now the Bore has its head, and it races towards the narrowing at Langney Sands where even with the risen water level the channel is just a few hundred yards across. Crashing, hissing, vicious and unstoppable, this is nature's lesson. We are not masters here; we are not even students. We are expendable.

It is catastrophic.

The bore is coming.

Sarah Dixon is a prolific writer of short stories where wonder plays an important role. A wife and mother of two, it was the desire to write stories that challenged the lure of video games that led her to write her first children's novel.

Now what?

David Zetland

We authors hope that these visions help you think of the various ways that climate change may impact your life — and the lives of everyone else in our world. Our advice is that you prepare for life in a different world as it's much easier to adapt to change than react to it. Besides considering your own actions, please also participate in your community's actions and preparations. Human civilization has brought us this far due to cooperation, and cooperation will be key to our futures.

This book is just the first in the ongoing Life Plus 2 Meters project. For our next stage, we're running a Kickstarter to raise money to fund prizes for the best visions contributed to *Life Plus 2 Meters (volume 2)*. If you want to support that project and/or want updates on the project's progress, then please visit `lifeplus2m.com`.

If you enjoyed this book, then please recommend it to friends and review it for others.

If you want to discuss anything about the project, then please email me at `dzetland@gmail.com`.

Thank you for reading!

Printed in Great Britain
by Amazon